A Teacher's Introduction to Philosophical Hermeneutics

College Section Committee

Tilly Warnock, Chair
University of Wyoming

Lil Brannon
SUNY at Albany

Doris O. Ginn, CCCC Representative
Jackson State University

Brenda M. Greene
Medgar Evers College, CUNY

Linda H. Peterson
Yale University

James F. Slevin
Georgetown University

Joseph F. Trimmer
Ball State University

Art Young
Clemson University

James Raymond, ex officio
University of Alabama

H. Thomas McCracken, CEE Representative
Youngstown State University

Janet Emig, Executive Committee Liaison
Rutgers University

A Teacher's Introduction to Philosophical Hermeneutics

Timothy W. Crusius
Southern Methodist University

NCTE Teacher's
Introduction Series

National Council of Teachers of English
1111 Kenyon Road, Urbana, Illinois 61801

To my father and mother,
Milton and Lois Crusius

Staff Editor: Sheila Ryan

Interior Design: Tom Kovacs for TGK Design

Cover Design: Joellen D. Bryant

NCTE Stock Number 50160-3050

Library of Congress Cataloging-in-Publication Data

Crusius, Timothy W., 1950-   .
    A teacher's introduction to philosophical hermeneutics / Timothy W. Crusius.
        p.   cm. — (NCTE teacher's introduction series, ISSN 1059-0331)
    Includes bibliographical references and index.
    ISBN 0-8141-5016-0
    1. Hermeneutics.   2. Rhetoric—Philosophy.   I. Title. II. Series.
BD241.C76   1991
121'.68'0248—dc20   91-34817
                                                                    CIP

Contents

Foreword

A Teacher's Introduction to Philosophical Hermeneutics is the second in what we hope will be a continuing series of books that are especially useful to teachers of English and language arts at all levels. Ours is a wide-ranging discipline, and important scholarly developments in various aspects of our field can be highly complex, not to mention voluminous. We often wish we had the time to take courses or do extended personal reading in topics such as deconstruction, psycholinguistics, rhetorical theory, and the like. Realistically, each of us can read intensively and extensively only in those areas that are of special interest to us or that are most closely related to our work. The Teacher's Introduction Series, then, is geared toward the intellectually curious teacher who would like to get an initial, lucid glance into rich areas of scholarship in our discipline.

Let me stress three things that are *not* intended in *A Teacher's Introduction to Philosophical Hermeneutics* and in future books that will appear in this series. First, the books are in no way shortcuts to in-depth knowledge of any field. Rather, these straightforward treatments are intended to provide introductions to major ideas in the field and to whet the appetite for further reading. Second, the books do not aim to "dumb down" complicated ideas, sanitizing them for an imagined "average reader." Many of the ideas are quite challenging, and we don't seek to patronize the reader by watering them down. Third, we don't want to send the message that every subject which is important to English and language arts teachers should be taught directly in the classroom. The personal enrichment of the teacher is paramount here. A great deal of misery might have been avoided in the 1960s if teachers had been doubly urged to learn about grammars new and old—that's part of being a well-rounded teacher—but to *avoid* bringing their new insights, tree diagrams and all, directly into the classroom.

We are grateful to Timothy Crusius for taking on the formidable work of writing so lucidly about the complexities of philosophical hermeneutics. We welcome your comments on the *Teacher's Introduction* concept.

Charles Suhor
Deputy Executive Director, NCTE

Preface

It is appropriate that a treatment of philosophical hermeneutics should follow Sharon Crowley's essay (1989) on deconstruction in NCTE's Teacher's Introduction Series. As a resolve "to read philosophers *in a certain way*" (Derrida 1989, 967, his emphasis), deconstruction is one way of interpreting texts and, therefore, in the most inclusive sense, a hermeneutic. And Derrida's work draws significantly from Martin Heidegger, the founder of philosophical hermeneutics.

The various intellectual struggles going on now within philosophy, theology, the social sciences, history, literary criticism, and rhetoric (among other fields) are in large measure a struggle over interpretation itself, what it should be and do. The major question is: How shall we receive—understand and evaluate—our own cultural heritage?

Shall we greet it with Nietzsche's "art of distrust," what Paul Ricoeur has called the "hermeneutics of suspicion" (1981, 63–64)? If so, hermeneutics becomes unmasking, primarily the dispelling of illusions and error, as not only in Nietzsche but also in Marx and Freud. Or shall we greet it in the spirit of the "hermeneutics of tradition" (1981, 64), seeing in history the sources of our own possibilities, of insights that no contemporary enlightenment can eclipse?

In his dismantlings of Western metaphysics, Derrida clearly belongs to the hermeneutics of suspicion; the theorist of chief concern here, Hans-Georg Gadamer, belongs to the hermeneutics of tradition.

As Ricoeur argues, the two hermeneutics are complementary rather than dichotomous (1981, 332). And yet, if we can speak of choice in matters governed so much by temperament, experience, and faith, choosing to emphasize one over the other is hardly a matter of indifference. If the choice amounts to a genuine commitment, it yields a way of living, because how we read texts, ourselves, other people, history, art—how we construe everything we encounter—largely determines what we do. For us, for English teachers, our hermeneutical emphasis plays a major role in what we teach, how we teach, and the thrust of our scholarly contributions. It matters profoundly, then, whether we incline toward deconstruction or philosophical hermeneutics, two of the major poststructural stances.

The following essay introduces philosophical hermeneutics to English teachers, with our role in writing instruction especially in mind. It is not a polemic in favor of Gadamer and against Derrida. Following Crowley's example, I have tried to be fair and balanced in sketching my subject, and I make no pretense to neutrality. Gradually, philosophical hermeneutics has become my philosophy of composition, informing both how I understand composing and how I teach it. So in trying to avoid polemics, I have not tried to avoid advocacy.

I gratefully acknowledge the work of John Paul Riquelme and Carolyn Channell, both of the Southern Methodist University English department, who gave the manuscript helpful readings. I also wish to thank James L. Kinneavy of the University of Texas, to whom I owe a great deal, including my first experience with philosophical hermeneutics. Finally, I am grateful for the stimulation and encouragement of Samuel B. Southwell of the University of Houston, who has been over the years my best friend, critic, and interlocutor.

Timothy W. Crusius
Southern Methodist University

Introduction

I believe that NCTE is to be highly commended for bringing out a book on hermeneutics for teachers. Hermeneutics, the art of interpretation, has preoccupied many of the best philosophical minds of the century: Martin Heidegger, Rudolf Bultmann, Jacques Derrida, Georg Gadamer, and Paul Ricoeur immediately come to mind. And Friedrich Nietzsche, Karl Marx, and Sigmund Freud from the last century have been highly influential names in hermeneutics also. Heidegger has been called by many the greatest philosopher of the twentieth century; his disciple, Bultmann, is considered by many to be the outstanding Christian theologian of this century; Gadamer, another of Heidegger's disciples, is also a major name in this century's list of philosophers. In the latter half of the century, Derrida would have to be mentioned as an imposing figure.

Despite the stature of these names and the fact that Heidegger's major work on hermeneutics was published sixty-four years ago and that E. D. Hirsch introduced hermeneutics to American scholarship thirty years ago, still it has not been a major formative influence on education generally or on English studies in particular. In English graduate courses, Derridean deconstruction did have a strong vogue for some time, but the general thrust of the discipline was not seriously changed, particularly in lower division college courses or at the high school level. At best, literary theory and criticism were affected, but certainly not rhetoric or composition.

Consequently, Timothy Crusius's book has to be welcomed as a serious attempt to bring twentieth-century philosophy to bear on the discipline of English, particularly in the field of rhetoric. Only two earlier works have attempted this marriage, both in the field of deconstruction. *Applied Grammatology: Post (e)-Pedagogy from Jacques Derrida to Joseph Beuys* (Baltimore: Johns Hopkins, 1984) was Gregory Ulmer's attempt to apply his view of deconstruction to writing theory, but it has not been very influential, possibly because it tended to emphasize some of the more bizarre aspects of deconstruction. In *A Teacher's Introduction to Deconstruction* (Urbana, Ill.: NCTE, 1989), Sharon Crowley conceded that, in the field of writing, deconstruction had little to offer the teacher, and she draws more directly from hermeneutics than from deconstruction in handling writing (53).

Consequently, Crusius is following Crowley's move, but enlarging the field of hermeneutics, especially to the trilogy of Heidegger, Gadamer, and Ricoeur. He considers these three as offering a positive hermeneutics. Conversely, although he adopts some perspectives from Nietzsche, Derrida, and modern Marxists, he follows Ricoeur in calling their theories "hermeneutics of suspicion," negative hermeneutics. In chapter 4 ("Why Philosophical Hermeneutics?"), Crusius juxtaposes philosophical hermeneutics to the hermeneutics of suspicion and argues, convincingly, I believe, that only the former can serve as a basis for contemporary rhetorical theory. In chapter 6, he considers the Marxist hermeneutics, which James Berlin has applied to rhetoric and composition. Crusius acknowledges many areas of agreement with philosophical hermeneutics, but also points out some critical differences.

From this full hermeneutic tradition, both positive and negative, Crusius has managed to extract and establish a solid philosophical foundation from contemporary philosophical theory for rhetoric and composition.

Crusius does this by explaining some of the important but formidable concepts of Heidegger and Gadamer in a plain style which consciously avoids philosophical jargon. This is no mean feat. His treatment of such notions as the primacy of Being over epistemology, of antifoundationalism, of being human (*Dasein*), of alienation, of thrownness, of projection, of forestructure, and of the hermeneutic circle are classic renditions of difficult philosophic concepts in language which ordinary people with college degrees can understand, given a little patience. Those who have struggled with these concepts in Gadamer, but especially in Heidegger, will be able to appreciate the relative simplicity of Crusius's presentation. With these concepts he erects a hermeneutic base for a rhetoric grounded in contemporary thought.

This hermeneutic makes no grand claim to a Truth which is eternal and inflexible (in this respect it is antifoundational). Nor does it claim to have the certainty of science. It is the interpretation theory of the humanities, the field of ethics, government, psychology, aesthetics, literature, and sociology. It considers the human being in his or her worldly situation, surrounded by cultural and situational influences which heavily determine major and minor decisions. It believes in freedom, but a freedom entrenched in cultural and situational circumstances. It believes that, in these freedom issues, scientific monological certainty is not a practical ideal; rather dialogue among people, with both or several sides having reasonable positions that necessitate compromises is the major communication tool. It believes that human beings are capable of achieving their projected visions, within the limits of the "worlds" they live in. It believes that probability, rather than truth, is the general rule in these areas, and that positions have constantly to be readjusted in the light of new evidence. This somewhat humble hermeneutic is the basis for Crusius's rhetorical theory.

The second part of the book is devoted to a sketch of the bases of this hermeneutic rhetoric. Crusius first joins hands with Marxist rhetoric in recognizing that all rhetoric is located within ideology. Berlin is the rhetorician whom he interfaces at this juncture. But Crusius then locates all ideologies within the forestructures, which he had established in the first part of the book. Thus rhetoric is located within his basic hermeneutic. This forestructure, unlike the Marxist ideology, he maintains, is capable of self-criticism.

He then applies the concept of forestructure to the rhetorical notion of invention, showing how much broader and far-reaching it is than the traditional rhetorical notion, especially as interpreted by some current rhetoricians. He argues that the hermeneutic notion of forestructure can give a serious philosophic base to the rhetorical notion of process. Chapter 7 is arguably the best section of the text. In it, Crusius interweaves nearly all of his hermeneutic concepts into a unified pedagogy, complete with several recent concrete examples of the methodology. And the style takes on a rhetorical seriousness worthy of the subject matter.

The examples which Crusius uses are all drawn from the domain of what he calls public discourse. He reasserts the claim that rhetoric should not be content free, as many modern rhetorics are, but that rhetoric should return to its original public concerns of politics, law, and related subjects. It is indeed true that rhetoric was born in the context of public discourse in Greece and Rome. And the church added religion to this context. So Crusius is here retrieving something of the heritage of classical rhetoric. Other rhetoricians are currently making the same claim. Michael Halloran, for example, has repeatedly told rhetorical scholars in English that they should imitate their confreres in departments of speech communications by insisting on the public discourse of rhetoric. This comes at the same time that new literary historians are insisting on the relevance of literature to the public discourse of the day.

Thus Crusius's hermeneutic rhetoric has serious connections with contemporary philosophic thought and with the influences which that thought are exerting in the literary segments of English departments. The book deserves a wide range of readers. It is relevant to the varied interest groups of English departments from rhetorical theory, history, and practice to literary theory, history, and practice. It can even provide a framework within which writing, linguistics, and literature can all live comfortably. And it is also relevant from the university down to the community college and school level.

James L. Kinneavy
University of Texas at Austin

I Philosophical
Hermeneutics:
Its Place and "Places"

1 A Typology;
Hermeneutics and Rhetoric

My focus is not hermeneutics in general, but specifically philosophical hermeneutics. To grasp the latter's significance requires the context of the former. And because, like rhetoric, hermeneutics has many meanings, we ought to survey some of them.

Five Interpretations of Interpretation

In its most common use, both now and in the past, hermeneutics designates the art or science of text interpretation. Writing preserves discourse over time and allows, especially with the advent of print, wide distribution over space. The inevitable result is some degree of alienation, as texts speak to a situation and an audience that no longer exist. "Hermeneutics has its origin in breaches of intersubjectivity" (Linge 1976, xii), breakdowns in both oral and written communication, but since texts cannot explain themselves, elaborate and self-conscious hermeneutical practice belongs to chirography and print. The need for it intensifies when a text such as sacred writ or legal codes has special authority and functions as a guide to decision-making. In such cases, we frequently interpret in the sense of construing intent—what, for example, the framers of the Constitution meant by establishing a religion—and by seeing current controversies in the light of our understanding of the past—for example, whether prayer in school amounts to establishing a religion.

For the greater part of its history, then, hermeneutics was really what is now sometimes called normative hermeneutics. When the dogma of the church is at stake in a culture where organized religion dominates daily activity or when a person's life, freedom, or property depends on the interpretation of statutes or precedent, a high premium accrues to having what will pass for correct and authoritative textual readings. In such circumstances, hermeneutics can become a highly specialized and esoteric pursuit.

Normative hermeneutics will always be with us. But in modern times the focus of concern has been on developing a scientific hermeneutics with a solid epistemological grounding. The spectacular development of natural science, whose methods seemed to yield certain and reliable knowledge, led students of the humanities and the social sciences to strive after equally precise and prestigious methods of inquiry and verification. However, when people study people they are studying history, not objects or natural processes that subjects can observe, but the very history in which subjects reside.

How, therefore, can we manage in the historical sciences to obtain the storied objectivity of the natural sciences? Only by resort, so scientific hermeneutics thought, to a methodical discipline as carefully controlled in its own way as natural science. The aim of scientific hermeneutics was to restore the past, which meant overcoming somehow the distance separating the object of study (for example, a text) from the subject or interpreter. Hence it relied heavily on philology, on efforts to reconstruct the world views of past eras, and on suspending all assumptions on the part of the interpreter that might distort restoration, recovery of the author's intention, and the original audience's understanding.

So conceived, hermeneutics would serve the epistemological needs of historical studies. It would produce reliable knowledge of the past. It would function as the foundational discipline of historical studies in much the same way that standards for data collection, experimental design, and statistical evaluation secure the authority of natural science.

Scientific hermeneutics is also still with us, very much alive, for example, in the work of Emilio Betti and E. D. Hirsch. Its assumptions and methods reign in journals dedicated to "hard scholarship." The two great founders of modern hermeneutics, Friedrich Schleiermacher and Wilhelm Dilthey, were after a scientific hermeneutics.

Philosophical hermeneutics radically questions the assumptions of scientific hermeneutics. Since Descartes, philosophy has been preoccupied with epistemological problems. Its basic questions are: How do we come to know anything? How can we be sure of what we claim to know? But epistemology tends to ignore a question prior to these: What is Being or beings? There is nothing to know and hence no problem of knowledge without beings—something to know about, someone capable of knowledge—hence the priority of the ontological over the epistemological question. In *Being and Time* (1962), Heidegger reasserted the priority of Being and provided the impetus for Gadamer's extensive development of philosophical hermeneutics in *Truth and Method* (1989b).

The specific concepts of philosophical hermeneutics are the concern of the next two chapters. In general it differs from both normative and scientific hermeneutics in its view of the status of interpretation. Interpretation is not primarily an art or a science, the special discipline of priests, lawyers, or professors; interpretation, rather, is human being, our mode of existence in the world. That is, hermeneutics does not come into play only when intersubjective understanding fails. It is not only an instrument for overcoming or preventing misunderstanding, as it was for Schleiermacher, or the enabling discipline of the human sciences, as it was for Dilthey. Rather, interpretation constitutes the world in which we exist. We always find ourselves in the midst of interpretations carried by our language and our culture. Regardless of our conscious stances toward history, we are caught up in history to a degree that we cannot hope to grasp or control fully. Because human being is being in time, "it"—what we try to objectify in scientific studies of language, culture, history, or tradition—is actually what "we"—supposedly neutral onlookers or subjects—are. To the extent that we can understand and interpret our intentions or actions, to proffer "readings" of this text or that individual's motives, we can do so because we always already dwell, mostly without being aware of it, in understandings, interpretations, and readings.

It follows that there is no subject "over here" and object "over there." Both belong to the history of interpretation. There is no place for a subject to stand outside or apart from this history-which-we-are, no neutral observing place, and no place where objects can appear apart from the history of understanding. It follows that knowledge can neither be discovered nor warranted by method. The whole rationale of scientific hermeneutics dissolves in Heidegger's hermeneutic of being.

All told we have

1. *Naïve or natural hermeneutics,* the spontaneous, everyday, mostly unreflective interpretations necessary when intersubjective understanding breaks down

2. *Normative hermeneutics,* the art of text interpretation as a deliberate and deliberating discipline for a "priestly" caste of specialists

3. *Scientific hermeneutics,* conceived as the foundational discipline of the human or historical sciences

4. *Philosophical or ontological hermeneutics,* a general philosophy of human existence, which holds that interpreting is not so much what human beings or some class of human beings do, but rather what all human beings are, namely, interpreters. To this typology we should add yet one more category, often called

5. *Negative or depth hermeneutics,* the hermeneutics of distrust or suspicion, a continuation of the Enlightenment's effort to liberate us from the dogma, error, and superstition of the past. It counters the emphasis of philosophical hermeneutics on being caught up, in Gadamer's phrase, "over and above our wanting and doing" (1989b, xxviii) in tradition. It is called "negative" because of its undermining intent and is sometimes styled "depth hermeneutics" because it purports to sound beneath linguistic surfaces to the unconscious (Freud) or to the economic-political conditions, the regimes of power, that control human communication (Marx, Nietzsche, Foucault).

The Priority of Philosophical Hermeneutics

Two basic questions remain in this initial survey of the territory: Why concentrate on philosophical hermeneutics? What does hermeneutics have to do with rhetoric?

Philosophical hermeneutics either subsumes, replaces, or claims priority to the other types. It subsumes naïve hermeneutics in that it aims to understand understanding itself. Philosophical hermeneutics is reflection on interpretation, a theory of what happens whenever we understand anything. It begins with a natural human ability or spontaneous performance, as does rhetoric, which strives to make conscious and accessible the process of speaking or writing well.

The relation of philosophical hermeneutics to the normative or negative types is more complex. It claims priority to any normative hermeneutic insofar as the interpretation of law, sacred texts, any body of art, and so on clearly depends on the general human ability to understand, whatever special assumptions or rules might distinguish, say, legal hermeneutics from biblical hermeneutics. To the extent that normative hermeneutics can rest only in "the" reading of some cultural artifact, philosophical hermeneutics denies such a possibility. For reasons that will become apparent in the next chapter, there can be no definitive reading of anything, no last or preemptive interpretation.

The concerns of philosophical hermeneutics are also indisputably prior to negative hermeneutics, since deconstructions depend on constructions, depths on surfaces, critiques on some existing self-understanding. But does philosophical hermeneutics subsume the various forms of negative hermeneutics? The claim of the latter rests in penetrating "beyond" or "beneath" natural hermeneutics and reflection on the process of interpretation itself. A good example is the

Marxist critique of ideology, which holds that interpretation is always distorted by economic and political inequities thought natural and ineluctable, whereas the inequities themselves are only the outcome of a temporary state in the means of production and therefore anything but beyond remedy. To detect the distortions, one must see through the rhetoric of apologists for the system to the real material conditions underpinning the system.

Neo-Marxian critics contend that philosophical hermeneutics lacks the systematic depth of ideology critique and thus is inadequate in itself both as a theory of interpretation and as a guide to constructive social change (Habermas 1986, 269–74). Gadamer contends that nothing inherent in philosophical hermeneutics excludes critical theory (1986, 288–89). But whether or not critique is subsumed by hermeneutics, the priority of understanding (for example, some construction of what a text says) to critique is enough in itself to justify concentration on the process of understanding.

Philosophical hermeneutics encompasses naïve hermeneutics and reflects on what is presupposed by the theory and practice of normative and negative hermeneutics. It may also replace scientific hermeneutics.

The energy once devoted to a science of interpretation has been dissipated by the failure of its proponents to advance a compelling method for stabilizing text interpretation. Too many of its key categories—"intention," for example—have become marginal in an intellectual climate very much aware of the impact of the un-, non-, and pre-conscious on all human activities. Moreover, the aspiration for certain knowledge in the human sciences to rival the natural sciences appears misplaced now that natural science itself is generally construed as a succession of paradigms, not a progressive refining of a single interpretation. Post-Kuhnian thought is no longer in awe of the natural sciences.

In Europe especially, but increasingly in this country as well, the assumptions of philosophical hermeneutics have displaced those of scientific hermeneutics. Why?

Philosophical hermeneutics begins explicitly with the primacy of Being, with our dependency on "the given," on nature, language, culture, tradition, and social practices. This starting point accords well with the social and ecological concerns of the age. Its basic postulate, human finitude, the limitations of temporal existence, recalls a broadly religious awareness. It also responds to the chastened aspirations of an age of specialists uncertain as to exactly where their work fits in the whole or even whether there is a whole for anything to fit in.

Habermas has ridiculed the self-conception of what he has called "the posties"—postmodern, poststructural, postanalytical, and so on. But he has also had to admit that the "master thinkers"—for example, Descartes, Kant, Hegel—have fallen on evil days (1987, 296). Precisely without claiming mastery, philosophical hermeneutics, with its stress on dialogue rather than system, is filling the void left by philosophy's foundational project—its attempt to establish an unshakeable ground of certain knowledge, now for the most part abandoned. In the absence of ultimates and absolutes, we are left with what Gadamer, echoing the German poet Hölderlin, called "the conversation that we ourselves are" (1989b, 378).

To a much greater extent than any other type of hermeneutics, philosophical hermeneutics is about the conversation that we are. Probably that is why it is moving to stage center even outside the humanities; that is why it deserves at least as much attention from us as deconstruction now enjoys. Deconstruction can reveal that scientific hermeneutics, in its effort to re-present a lost presence, to restore a past meaning, is but another instance of the metaphysics of presence; it can, that is, critique scientific hermeneutics, but cannot offer anything positive as an alternative. Philosophical hermeneutics can. It is, to use John Dewey's term, "reconstructionism," the necessity and value of which Crowley recognizes by frankly admitting that, in her suggestions for teaching writing, she has shifted from deconstruction proper to hermeneutics (1989, 53). To compose (from *componere,* to put together) is to construct and reconstruct, interpret and reinterpret; deconstruction can at most be a moment within this process, not an end in itself.

Hermeneutics and Rhetoric: Relationships

The close relation between rhetoric and hermeneutics has been explicitly recognized for a long time. At least since Schleiermacher it is a commonplace that the two verbal arts are complementary—text-making, text interpretation (Palmer 1969, 88). Gadamer, however, points to rhetoric's claim to priority in the sense that "by its very nature [rhetoric is] antecedent to hermeneutics in the limited sense [of text interpretation] and . . . represents something like the positive pole to the negative of textual explication" (1989a, 276). In rhetoric, something is put together and comes to stand; only by this "first" can the answering "second" of interpretation take place.

Habermas agrees with Gadamer, while also calling attention to the common origin of rhetoric and hermeneutics "in arts which take in hand the methodical training and development of a natural ability. The art of interpretation is the counterpart of the art of convincing and persuading in situations where practical questions are brought to decision" (Habermas 1989, 294).

When we think of hermeneutics in the limited sense of text interpretation, the linkage with rhetoric tends to remain external, as if the two were sharply distinct arts. But Habermas's reference to practical questions suggests a deeper, more integrated connection, which Gadamer explicates in the following way:

> Where else . . . should theoretical reflection on the art of understanding turn than to rhetoric, which from the earliest days of the tradition has been the sole champion of a claim to truth which vindicates the plausible, the *eikos* (verisimilar), and that which is illuminating to common sense against science's claim to proof and certainty? To convince and illuminate without being able to prove, that clearly is just as much the goal and measure of understanding and explication as it is of rhetoric and the art of persuasion. (1989a, 279)

Here we detect the goal shared by the two arts, to hold open a notion of truth that is neither self-evident nor reducible to methodical verification. Most of our questions are practical ones in the art of daily living—questions that can neither be approached by nor await the labors of method, but must be decided now on the basis of common sense and the most plausible interpretation, or the most persuasive argument. This Aristotelian notion of truth as *pistis* (opinion, faith) is therefore really the one that dominates human affairs. Chaim Perelman's *The New Rhetoric* (1969) is about this notion of truth, as is Wayne Booth's *Modern Dogma and the Rhetoric of Assent* (1974).

There remains at least one more level, deeper still, where, in Gadamer's words, "the rhetorical and the hermeneutical aspects of human linguisticality interpenetrate each other at every point" (1989a, 280). At this level, hermeneutics is no longer primarily a natural ability taken in hand and turned into a partly conscious art, a faculty cultivated for interpreting texts. Rather, hermeneutics is ontological, Heidegger's *Dasein*, human-being-in-the-world. We do not employ rhetoric and hermeneutics as we select a tool for this or that purpose; we are, in our very being, persuaders and interpreters, beings immersed in language and dwelling in a world both made and revealed by language. It follows that there is no first; the rhetorician's act is interpretation and interpretation an act of rhetoric. At this level, the level of philosophical or ontological hermeneutics, rhetoric and hermeneutics come together in a dialogue of mutual reflection.

The rest of this essay is an effort to begin this dialogue, first by meditating on the recurrent *topoi* of philosophical hermeneutics, and then by letting its "places" become the region for a rethinking of rhetoric. Why a rethinking? As Gadamer explains,

> There would be no speaker and no act of speaking if understanding and consent were not in question, were not underlying elements; there would be no hermeneutical task if there were no mutual understanding that has been disturbed and that those involved in the conversation must search for and find again. It is a symptom of our failure to realize this and evidence of the increasing self-alienation of human life in our modern epoch when we think in terms of organizing a perfect and perfectly manipulated information—a turn modern rhetoric seems to have taken. In this case, the sense of mutual interpenetration of rhetoric and hermeneutics fades away and hermeneutics is on its own. (1976b, 25–26)

Perhaps better than anyone else, Derrida has revealed the impossibility and the hubris of a perfect and perfectly manipulated information. It is a dream for machines, not people. If we rethink rhetoric hermeneutically, perhaps we can do something about one modern alienation and revive the conversation between rhetoric and hermeneutics.

2 *Topoi* I: Homelessness and Being

> The real question is not in what way being can be understood
> but in what way understanding is being.
> —Gadamer 1976b, 49

To understand a philosophy is to acquire a language, not so much in the sense of a glossary of terms, a set of categories, but more in the sense of *topoi,* the generative commonplaces of its thinking. "Commonplace" is especially appropriate in the case of philosophical hermeneutics with its emphasis on an existential vocabulary rather than a technical jargon. Instead of talk of axioms and corollaries and entailments, implicatures, propositions, illocutionary acts, and the like, philosophical hermeneutics uses a vocabulary that stays as close as possible to general human experience and the common problems of understanding. It is a terminology less suited for analysis than for *inventio,* for further discoveries, a language that would listen to rather than dissect the things of an objective world or the propositions of somebody's utterances. In this most of all, hermeneutics shows its debt to rhetoric.

The way I discuss hermeneutics here will perhaps not please a certain scholarly disposition. With few exceptions, I have not given the German originals of the key terms and phrases, since only a thorough familiarity with German could make them meaningful. Those who have familiarity do not need the German words; those who lack it will scarcely find the German terms helpful. Nor have I been rigorous in discriminating Heidegger from Gadamer or either from Ricoeur. The result, I hope, is a compact, uncluttered, accessible rendering of mainly Gadamer's version of philosophical hermeneutics. I readily admit, however, that my approach obscures the differences among these three thinkers, differences both numerous and significant. Finally, I should warn the reader that I have been selective in choosing what to discuss and what to discuss in relative detail. For the most part, I have not even alluded to the great·deal left out or explained why some aspects receive special attention. Space will not permit the former; the latter is determined by my perception of the concerns of English teachers.

Homelessness

> Foxes have holes, and birds of the air have nests; but the Son of
> man has nowhere to lay his head.
>
> —Matthew 8:20

One central theme of contemporary thought is spiritual crisis. Something has gone badly wrong with the ways of the West, despite its relative wealth and its domination of global affairs. So pervasive is this theme that one finds diagnoses of and prescriptions for the malaise underlying our frantic activity almost everywhere, in a host of sources seeming to share little else but the theme itself.

Heidegger characterized our era as "the darkening," glossed as "the flight of the gods, the destruction of the earth, the transformation of men into a mass, [and] the hatred of everything free and creative" (1977a, 37–38). He did not offer much in the way of advice, apparently because of an almost Greek-like resignation to fate, but he did try to bring light to the darkening by striving to understand the sources of rootlessness and alienation. How did we arrive where we are? How is it that there is so little sense of belonging to anything, that even the fortunate residing in energy-efficient suburban houses find no home, no authentic dwelling place?

For Heidegger, for Derrida, and before both of them, for Nietzsche, the problem is metaphysics, whose heritage extends from Plato. Truth for Plato is the ancient ideal of theory, silent contemplation of the eternal, the *eidos* (form). Here is the source of the dispassionate Western onlooker and the object or thing concept of being—of the subject-object dichotomy, prominent in Western thought to this day. Scientific method is wholly dependent on it, as is the applied science of technology. For modern thought the source is Descartes, whose philosophy turns on a finally unbridgeable hiatus between mind and thing. But it is just as evident in Kant, who wanted to know exactly what the mind contributes to knowledge as opposed to the objects the mind experiences. And even Hegel, whose struggle is to overcome the subject-object dichotomy, affirms its centrality in the very struggle to overcome it.

Homelessness is the inevitable outcome of subject-object thinking. The contemplative self is an alienated self. It does not belong to the earth, to "the works and days of hands," for the earth is a realm of alteration and anything that changes can at best be a shadow of the real. The earth is appearance, illusion, death, or as the preacher said, vanity (emptiness). This self does not belong to history, for the contemplative mind wants most of all a world of abstract law, fixed regularity, whose jurisdiction is universal and potentially ideal, completely knowable and predictable. Truth does not belong to time, and insofar as we pursue "the Truth," neither do we. It does not belong to society, to the active life of practical affairs, the life of rhetoric and discussion, for this life is caught up in earth and history and messy contingency and imprecision and mere opinion and endless controversy—in everything the contemplative merely tolerates, ignores, or despises.

The contemplative self, in sum, is self-alienated, shorn of what he or she is. A mind purified for pure reason cannot fully acknowledge its bodily home either. The flesh is transitory and therefore of little consequence, or it is the source of weakness and evil. All that finite and fallible human beings are—flesh, earth, creatures of time, who belong to a particular place, society, and language—is rejected in favor of a dwelling *meta-physis,* beyond nature. The Son of (wo)man, the prophet, the role now filled by the scientist and the technocrat, has no place to rest his head because his places are no-places, utopias of mathematics, technical languages, symbolic logics, "heavens" of pure form with or without God. The great imperative is to find the source or ground of "the" one Truth, the foundational project of Western philosophy; the lesser imperatives are abstract and analyze, explain, predict, and, where possible, shape and manipulate to satisfy human desires. Method and technique, the god-terms of mastery, are the idols of the West, especially the modern West, yielding in our time the cult of the expert, the bureaucratic Leviathan, global domination by international business, and lives dedicated to self-improvement (even the self is manipulatable) and temporary arrangements, rootlessness made almost obligatory and certainly normal (a move on average every three to four years; a flitting here and a flitting there in the cause of business or recreation).

In our world there is little sense of locale; in the language of metaphysics, alienation and homelessness are not incidental or accidental but essential to modernity. For this reason, no serious hermeneutical thinker imagines an easy overcoming of the subject-object dichotomy or a sudden recovery of a sense of belonging. To employ a distinction put to another use by Frank Lentricchia in *Criticism and Social Change* (1983, 50–51), we can demystify the condition in which we find ourselves, to some extent understanding it; but defusing it, doing something about the power it has over us, is quite another matter. We may, for example, grasp clearly the dangers of the technological compulsion to control nature, but we look for solutions in still more technology, as in the various proposals for disposing of nuclear wastes.

For Heidegger, modernity is a fate, the destiny of our way of being, which must simply run its course. He did refer to "the turning" (1977b, 39–42), a future point when we can enter a new way of being. For Heidegger, this turning is something we cannot make happen, but something that will happen to us, perhaps something that is happening to us as we try to imagine a postmodern existence, for the most part conceived negatively, as only the antithesis of modernity.

For Heidegger, Gadamer, and Ricoeur—who differ sharply on this count with Derrida and with another influential French philosopher, Jean-François Lyotard, author of *The Postmodern Condition* (1984)—there can be no revolutionary break with the past, no sudden shifting of ground. Whatever possibilities we have reside in understanding our own history, not in leaping to somewhere else. It is accurate, then, to call philosophical hermeneutics profoundly conservative. But its critique of metaphysics also reveals an emancipatory interest that clearly sets it apart from an uncritical traditionalism. There is no simple endorsement of what we are.

Philosophical hermeneutics does not believe that it can decree an end to modernity or overcome metaphysical self-alienation by deconstructing the subject-object dichotomy or any of the other habitual distinctions of Western thought. Its program is more modest and, I would argue, more realistic. The ways of living and thinking that result in homelessness are deeply entrenched in our social practices, our institutions, and especially in our language, all of which operate for the most part preconsciously. Interpretation—hermeneutical reflection—can bring only bits of what is going on to awareness. Even when it does, not only must it reckon with never having the whole picture, but also with resistance or denial, in the strong Freudian sense of these words, and less dramatically with loss of insight through daily immersion in the business of our lives. Emancipation is consequently slow and imperfect, caught up as we are in a finite existence prestructured by the tremendous inertial force of the past, whose effects on us are both good and bad, typically at the same time.

All philosophical hermeneutics can hope to do, therefore, is hold open an alternative, constantly pointing to ways of living and thinking less destructive of the earth and the human spirit. The pervasive way we have thought about being, as consisting of isolatable objects that can be technologically manipulated, willed to be what we want them to be, is not the only way of thinking about being or living in the world.

Philosophical hermeneutics is an effort to rethink what we are and how we might relate ourselves to the world. It is preparation for and complicity with the turning, when perhaps we can learn to heed the claims of Being.

The Priority of Being

Western thought since Descartes typically begins with an individual consciousness contrasted with what it can be conscious of, the objects of contemplation or experience. Truth can only be correspondence or correctness, a perfect match between the "in here" (what we assert about the world) and the "out there" (objective existence). Philosophical hermeneutics does not deny consciousness. It does not deny that some experiences can be objectivized, treated as so many self-contained items. It does not deny the legitimacy of human concern, within some frame of reference, for reporting the world accurately. What it does deny is the primacy of the subject-object dichotomy.

Before subjects can be observers of and asserters about the world, they must be dwellers within it. The Western subject belongs to the world from which it would abstract itself. It "knows" the world tacitly, preconsciously, always to a much greater extent than it knows in the sense of explicit formulation. Our being-in-the-world, then, is always prior to abstracting (literally "drawing away from") this being-in-the-world to become the Cartesian *cogito*. Prearticulate experience and semiconscious know-how gained from interacting with the environment condition both what and how we observe, so that the neutral, disinterested subject is at best, by the most charitable construction, an unattainable ideal.

We do not and cannot exist as an isolated, individual mind or consciousness. We belong to a society and a culture in the sense of unquestioning interiorization of its norms and ways long before we have the capacity to reflect and criticize. The very fiction of the detached subject is itself a cultural norm, not a natural fact or an ineluctable beginning point or postulate. This fiction conceals too much our being-with-others, which always underlies the act of will required to function, temporarily and imperfectly, as mere onlookers. And because it conceals the more deeply rooted being-with-others, it also conceals the moral imperatives that guide observation. We cannot just look; we are always looking for something, something made significant by the explicit and tacit rules of the game, for what counts within some particular inquiry or context.

The subject side, then, of the subject-object dichotomy is neither primary nor self-aware. It cannot be what it claims to be: apart from the world, whereas it is always in the middle of things; isolated, whereas it is always more collective and social than individual.

What about the other side, the side of the object? As the epistemological subject is a reification, so also is the object of its gaze. In the first place, as Edmund Husserl clearly showed, we can focus on some one something only by ignoring the context or background against which we perceive it (Gadamer 1976b, 118). No less than subjects, objects exist only in the middle of things. In the second place, any perceiving is always a "seeing as," not the pure seeing, the "just looking" of naïve empiricism. Since to perceive an individual tree as *tree* requires the concept *tree*, language conditions perception at a mostly deep, nonconscious level.

The phrase "priority of Being" sums up the hermeneutical critique of Cartesian epistemology. The separation of subject from object amounts to a forgetting of their belonging together in the world, in Being. Heidegger's famous hammer analogy in *Being and Time* (1962, 69) expresses the relationship clearly. For the carpenter, the hammer is an extension of the hand, an existential unity, bound together in purposefulness, the project at hand. The hammer can become an object only when it falls out of human projects—when the hammer breaks, for example. Our knowledge of the hammer is rooted in our unreflective use of it; we know it as such only when it ceases to function in our world, when it ceases to be a hammer. Subject-object thinking treats all experience as if it were broken, as if the belonging together of people and things that always precedes the momentary abstractions to subject and object were unimportant.

"Thinking Being" is the step back from subjects and objects to the more original relationship of existential unity. To use Kenneth Burke's geological metaphor (1969a, xix), consciousness becomes only the crusts thrown up from the molten center of Being, where all exists as the not-yet-distinguished; objectivity becomes but one possible stance of no special privilege; and truth as correspondence becomes secondary to the question of how anything comes to appearance at all.

That is: before we can make any judgments about a tree, before any statements about objects are possible, the tree must somehow show itself to us, come out of the molten center as tree. But how? That question belongs to the next *topos*.

Being as Event

"Being as event" is the place of places for philosophical hermeneutics. Much of its vocabulary was designed to talk about Being nonsubstantially—that is, not as perduring sameness, as the eternal Is, but as happening, something that occurs in time and in this world. Philosophical hermeneutics asserts the priority of Being as a counter to the alienation of human being from the world, of subjects from objects, and as a way of displacing consciousness from the center of modern Western thought; it asserts Being as event as an alternative to the fixation with objective truth, which always alienates the knower from the known and restricts truth itself to either self-evidence or the methodically verified.

The rest of the *topoi* discussed in the next chapter have to do with Being as event, not with truth as correctness or correspondence of a proposition with an extraverbal state of affairs, but with truth as disclosure or unconcealedness, how beings "show themselves" to us. It is therefore crucial that we understand what Being means—and perhaps more important, what it does not mean—in the context of hermeneutics and why hermeneutics insists on the temporality of Being and truth over the "eternal truths" termed objective.

Although there have always been significant dissenting voices, Western philosophy has on the whole tried to think being in two ways. In the first way, being inheres in the things of experience and gives them identity. There is, for example, a "treeness" about trees, and even a "goodness" about everything we call good. Being is the search for essence; the only question is whether we have the right concepts for saying what a tree or the good is. In other words, whatever is isolatable in experience has a fixed nature, whose essence is in principle knowable. This or that tree will deteriorate, die, and return to the earth, but the essence of tree will live on in timeless statements about treeness. To assume otherwise is to fall into sophistry, to say, as indeed the Sophists did say, that what is good depends on whether one is talking to Athenians or Spartans.

This way of thinking attends to the Being of beings and works with a propositional calculus—that is, with concepts combined into assertions. Its characteristic tool is logic. Its philosophical concern is with validity—the formal correctness of statements and sets of statements —and with truth in the sense of correspondence or extension, the extralinguistic state of affairs represented by concepts and statements. It is metaphysical in the sense that it assumes a stable order that is not only accessible to reason, but is in its very being *logos*, rational.

For the most part, Western thought has been preoccupied with the Being of beings, with intellectual and technical mastery of things. But it has also sought to grasp the Being of beings in a second way, not as the treeness of tree, but as the "isness" of tree, the Being that any existent thing shares with all existing things. Here, the attempt of Western thought to reach "beyond nature" becomes most obvious: Plato's *eidos*, Aristotle's unmoved mover, the Hellenized God of the New Testament, and all their many variations and derivatives testify to the metaphysical ground or foundation attributed to Being itself. Being in this version is not only beyond shape-shifting appearance, but is also beyond flesh and earth in some heavenly or transcendent realm of pure intellection and imperishable Being.

Western thought is driven to the metaphysical strategem because it wants to grasp Being in the same way that it grasps everything else, conceptually. But the concept of Being is empty, contentless, indistinguishable from Nothing. If one tries to think of Being itself apart from anything that exists, one finds only nullity, for isness offers nothing concrete for the mind to grasp. All that can be said about Being is that it is not: not limited, not mortal, not anything that belongs to our experience, our world. It therefore has to be metaphysical, like the God whose perfect circular nature has its center everywhere and its circumference nowhere. Only in such paradoxical metaphors can Being itself find conceptual expression.

In sum, then, the Western effort to think being ends in either the will to power, domination of beings, or in a Being so refined that not even breath or wind can represent it. Both result from the conceptual reduction of being; they belong together, as hubris and emptiness belong together.

By Nietzsche's time, if not before, metaphysics' way of thinking being was anachronistic. Evolutionary thought destroyed whatever was left of the idea of a stable chain of being, and with it the Being of beings as essence. Beings can still be thought as structure and structural transformation (that is, process), but not as essence in the sense of a permanent, inherent nature. At the same time, the hold of a realm beyond this world, whether sustained by a personal, theistic God or the abstract God of the philosophers, was slipping. Any positing of a realm beyond nature triggers suspicion as a sign of bad faith or inauthenticity, the choice of comforting illusions over solid effort in this world now.

For the most part, the old ontological question of the Being of beings is just not asked. In the context of modernity, it is hard to dispute Heidegger's accusation that Western thought has forgotten Being

(1977a, 41). At the same time, a century after Nietzsche, it is no longer interesting, much less prophetic, to announce the end of metaphysics. If, as some say, deconstruction has lost vitality, probably that loss results from its job being done. What is left of the metaphysics of presence that needs deconstruction? Disorganized remnants survive in popular culture and can still undergird reactionary political programs—as will to power, we still have to take it seriously—but I can think of no important contemporary advocate of truth as unmediated presence. The genuine issue now is not whether or how to bring metaphysics to an end. Metaphysics is spent. The issue, rather, as Robert Nozick put it, is to find a place worth being (1981, 2). The issue is living meaningfully.

To find a place worth being can hardly be managed with thinking that forgets place and being. By a kind of internal necessity, traditional Western thought deprived us of both through obsession with objectivity, universals, and absolutes, nonplaces where no one can dwell. But have the antitraditional and nontraditional alternatives opened a place worth being? Some have looked to the East, exotic and fascinating, no doubt, but not a home for Western minds. Others have sought a place worth being in some future fruition, like the classless state, long recognized as a materialistic parody of the Kingdom of God on earth. Like the Kingdom of God, such a faith seems to reside in endless deferral, the difference between Derrida's world of infinite signifiers and the prophetic never-quite-yet being that the former cannot imagine a signified. Others see the new age as here already in the form of a definitive break with the past. Henceforth we are free to make and remake ourselves at will. "But out of what?" one might ask. Presumably, like the God of metaphysics, out of nothing, for if the past does not carry our possibilities, what does? Being as radical freedom seems indistinguishable from freedom as "just another word for nothing left to lose," to recall a poignant definition from a once-popular song.

Philosophical hermeneutics' effort to rethink Being as event eludes easy categorization as traditional or anti/nontraditional, modern or postmodern. On the one hand, reviving Being seems to run counter to the aggressive nihilism of post-Nietzschean thought as well as the implicit nihilism of scientific-technical reason, which does not think Being at all. Philosophical hermeneutics "reaches back," trying to recover something lost by both sides in the current struggle between modern and postmodern allegiances.

And yet, on the other hand, philosophical hermeneutics is not traditional in the hapless "back to" kind of thinking characteristic of nostalgia for some lost golden age. No less than Nietzsche, philosophical hermeneutics breaks with metaphysics. Being is not something open to conceptual grasp and control. Being always has us; we always find ourselves within not just a natural environment, but a world, a particular society, language, history. In this world, the life-situation of our time and place, Being *is* in the sense of established social practices and institutions, prevailing interpretations of what has been, is, and can be; but Being also unfolds in the sense that interpretation never stops, can never reach finality. If we belong to Being in that we cannot step aside from or discard our society, language, or history, we also "make Being" through the reflective power of language, through partial deconstructions and reconstructions of understandings passed down to us.

As we make our way through some of the *topoi* of Being as event, we might think about philosophical hermeneutics as a whole in the context of postmodernism. Philosophical hermeneutics is postmodern in that it does not pretend to know anything about ultimate foundations and final or ultimate Truth. But in rejecting the Being of metaphysics, it does not reject Being, as postmodernism generally does. The key move of philosophical hermeneutics is to construe Being in time, as the truths of process and discovery rather than essence and correctness, of unsecured imaginative insight rather than system and method. Being is the immanent, the always emerging meanings concealed when tradition is reified, made into what it is not, monolithic and static. The place worth being is participation in the truths now unfolding, in the revealing and making-remaking of Being itself. It is a certain activity, a way of being, not a state of being.

3 *Topoi* II: *Dasein* and Dialogue

The real power of hermeneutical consciousness is to see what is questionable.

Reality happens within language.

—Gadamer 1976b, 13, 35

Traditional hermeneutics (that is, text interpretation) seeks to overcome the alienation of writing, to restore as full a meaning as possible to linguistic structures estranged from context and voice. Philosophical hermeneutics goes beyond specifically textual alienation to the alienation of human being from Being. This more general, ontological concern is part of what makes philosophical hermeneutics philosophical.

It also merits the name as a critique of mainstream Western philosophy. Metaphysics sets Being against and elevates it over existence; philosophical hermeneutics counters with an existential Being that can no longer be thought as a dichotomy or as a doctrine of two worlds. Epistemology sets subject against object and oscillates between the two, sometimes valuing only the latter, reducing truth to naturalistic-objectivist parameters, sometimes valuing only the former, extolling subjective truth as the only truth that matters. Philosophical hermeneutics advances the world-revealing, world-creating power of language—"the house of Being," Heidegger called it (1977b, 193)—as the source of all knowledge and truth.

So-called subjects, human beings, live always immersed in the symbols and language of the culture or tradition that they—or rather, we—embody. Therefore, we can only know ourselves hermeneutically by interpretation, through "reflection . . . [on] the opaque, contingent, and equivocal signs scattered in the cultures in which our language is rooted" (Ricoeur 1970, 47). So-called objects likewise exist for us only as mediated by language. It is idle to speculate about what a tree is "in itself," for we can know it only as "tree," as a structure of many substructures revealed by the analytical terminology of science or as a rich symbol of our dreams and art.

No less than subjects, objects are known hermeneutically, as interpretations and through reflection on interpretations. There is nothing that can be known or understood about either subjects or objects before interpretation or beyond interpretation, outside a symbolically constituted experience. Or as Gadamer succinctly and memorably put it, "Being that can be understood is language" (1989b, 474). This formula eliminates epistemology's abstract and artificial hiatus between subjects and objects. Subjects and objects dwell together in the house of Being; both are known through the Being-event of language.

The above comments amount to another way of traversing the same territory negotiated thus far and especially in the previous chapter: homelessness, the priority of Being, and Being as event. The *topoi* of this chapter amount to developments of Being as event, an effort to think it more precisely and in greater detail.

Dasein and Authenticity

Western thought about human being is summed up in Hamlet's indecision between two alternatives: "how like an angel . . . quintessence of dust." On the one hand, as spirit, human being belongs to its heavenly origin and source, to God or the Logos, Reason. On the other hand, as flesh, human being is Adam, earth, dust fated to return to dust. At the level of human reflection on the human, we see the metaphysical struggle between Being and existence bifurcating everything, including humanity's understanding of itself. The opposition is still with us in the form of conventional Christianity's hope for individual salvation and/or the advent of the Kingdom of God versus Darwin's view of human being as just another animal species.

Dasein, usually translated as "human existence" or "human-being-in-the-world," would seem an unambiguous decision for "Dust thou art, and unto dust thou shalt return." As Heidegger develops it in *Being and Time* (1962), *Dasein* is not the abstraction "human existence," but rather concrete or authentic human existence, akin to the stark, anxiety-ridden realism of the Old Testament. "Man [and woman, for on this count there is perfect equality] goeth to his [her] long home," the grave, and lives authentically only in the face of death. Heidegger's Being, like Yahweh once he has shaken off his origin as a tribal God and becomes the one God, is everywhere and inescapable, embracing human being. *Dasein* belongs to Being in the profound and precarious way that Israel—and through Israel, all the nations—belongs to Yahweh.

But we must not push the analogy too far. *Dasein's* contemporary, existential flavor derives from groundlessness. *Dasein* always finds itself within Being; insofar as it remains authentic, it cannot claim an assured origin or fate. Being is the opening or clearing, the frames of meaning within which all beings, including human being, reveal themselves. Being is therefore not God in the cosmos-sustaining sense, but intensely local, historical, bound to time and place, to this language and culture's (or subculture's) world interpretation. Hence, although Old Testament figures sometimes fear that Yahweh has turned his back on them and frequently complain about his delays in securing their desires, the thought that Yahweh might not be there at all is unthinkable. Hermeneutical Being can be thought either with or without God, in trusting faith or nihilistically. But *Dasein* must acknowledge its ignorance about ultimates and absolutes. Authentic human existence cannot avoid the question of grounding, but it also cannot rest in a warranted answer.

There can be no question, however, of the central, humbling intent of *Dasein:* We are not masters of Being. At the same time, Heidegger allows us a special function closed to the naturalistic conception of humanity as only a species amid species. We are the being for whom Being is an issue, a question; we are the being that interrogates the meaning of both existents and existence. We care about it; it matters to us. And this is the task of authentic *Dasein,* the caring and the questioning, a determination neither to opt for metaphysical consolations nor to allow ourselves to be totally absorbed into "they," into the everyday chattiness of a life made safe by trivialization.

Dasein is hardly angelic. It seems, however, that Being has picked us out to speak for it—a quintessence of dust with language, then. And in and through language a *Mitsein*, being with others, "they" for the most part in conducting our daily affairs, but occasionally really alive in the passion for questioning.

Thrown-Projection

The key to understanding *Dasein* is not to confuse it either with individual subjectivity or with humankind, the nearly contentless abstraction. Both of these more familiar notions attempt to avoid Being's temporal structure, the former by positing a unique, unchanging self, the latter by moving to an almost empty category. Both belong, that is, to metaphysics, which is hostile to time and change. Both seek an essence, some fixed core of being. But Being and *Dasein* in philosophical hermeneutics are first and last historical and therefore contingent, always about to become not quite foreseeably different. The radical contingency of *Dasein* is stressed in Heidegger's *topos* of thrown-projection (1977a, 64–65).

The previous section called attention to the groundless or unsecured quality of human existence. It is precisely the cloud of unknowing obscuring both ultimate origins and final destinations that attracts us to the foundational project of metaphysics. We want answers, not questions, something definite and sustaining above or beneath, before and after the arc of existence. All we can know, however, is the anxiety of thrown-projection.

We are *thrown* by the circumstances of birth into the life-world of our time and place. This life-world—not the neutral world of science, objectified into observable objects and processes—is tradition, Being, an evolving horizon of meanings that prestructures everything we encounter. It makes us to a much greater degree than we make it; we are always already living a preinterpreted existence, long before any capacity for sustained critique develops and still for the most part after the onset of mature judgment.

Being or tradition, then, is our "ground." It is quite groundless in its constant alteration and has no "first place," but rather retreats towards and is finally lost in what Shakespeare's Prospero called "the dark backward and abysm of time." Moreover, it is no single, unified structure, but a complex of unstable and heterogeneous survivals— voices, institutions, practices, texts, and so on—ungraspable as a totality and fraught with possibilities.

The mention of possibility suggests *projection*, the complement of "thrownness." Our lives are shaped not only by the present, a sedimentation of the past, but also by our projects and projections, our willing of the future. If thrownness designates intricacy with Being beyond our willing and doing, projection is *Dasein's* retort to Being, if always within and limited by Being. That is, we make and remake ourselves through activity, in small but significant ways altering both what we are and the explicating of Being itself. The process is dialectical. Being is not a set of objects or processes that we can manipulate at will, nor is it the vast, indifferent universe that renders all human action absurd. Rather, as the understanding that always precedes us, Being exists only for us and as us; as the being that cares and questions, we have a say in (if not a say over) Being. Total freedom, total self-determination is both illusory and empty; but in our existence as interpretation we can and do reinterpret received views and even reinterpret interpretation itself. We participate in Being.

The relationship is asymmetrical—Being always has priority—but is still reciprocal, for a change in *Dasein's* self-understanding alters Being as well. Philosophical hermeneutics does not leave us in the position of powerless victims, as does so much contemporary thought that also displaces the subject-agent as the prime mover.

Finitude

Being is inexhaustible. We can and do go on unpacking the meanings of symbols scattered in the world without ever arriving at "the" interpretation. There is always more to say because the spontaneous symbols of natural language, dreams, art, religious rituals, and the like are polysemous and because the horizon or context within which we understand them is always changing. Being, therefore, is unbounded but not absolute because historical, temporal, and contingent. We must continually remind ourselves that the Being of philosophical hermeneutics is not the Being of metaphysics, of perduring presence or underlying, fixed essence, or all-inclusive but empty abstraction. Rather, Being is the dynamic life-world into which are thrown willy-nilly at birth.

Hermeneutical Being does not promise complete intellectual possession or practical control of anything. The illusion of mastery shared by metaphysics and scientific-technical reason is rather the unwisdom of the West, which philosophical hermeneutics would dispel. We must learn to think and live without it, not just because it is self-deceptive, but more importantly because it is horribly destructive. Human being that would be God is the heart of darkness; but human being that knows only that it belongs to Being and that, like Socrates, cares and questions within an understanding of its ignorance is the place worth being.

Because *Dasein* belongs to Being, it too is inexhaustible, infinite in the nonabsolute way of Being. We never complete the explicating of ourselves. But as individual thrown projects, our being is radically finite. The thoughtful person strives for self-knowledge; however, as Gadamer remarks, "to be historically means that knowledge of oneself can never be complete" (1989b, 302). When the will to mastery runs finally against limitation—if only its own mortality—it falls into despair. In contrast, *Dasein,* authentic human-being-in-the-world, is *Mitsein,* being with others and otherness, which always implies finitude and always requires us to "let being be," not merely in the negative sense of tolerating difference, but in the positive sense of listening for the insights of the other.

In hermeneutical activity, with its openness to dialogue, the metaphysical despair of the always collapsing system, the "one Truth" continually giving way to yet another "one Truth," is at length overcome. Plenty of opportunity remains, however, for hermeneutical despair—in the closed mind, in the totalitarian enforcing of the one Truth. Re-cognition of what wisdom has always known, that to be human is to be finite, is at least a step toward acknowledging the conversation which we are.

Preunderstanding and the Circle

The premise upon which philosophical hermeneutics stands or falls is that there is nothing for *Dasein* that falls outside of interpretation. "Reality happens within language," within Being or the life-world enabled by language.

Philosophical hermeneutics affirms the realist assumption of extramental existence; it is not idealism, which holds that all existence depends on the mind or will of God (Berkeley) or equates spirit with the world process (Hegel). Philosophical hermeneutics denies the positivist view that we can have an unmediated—that is, a symbol-free or language-free—access to the extramental world. Reality is not only language; reality happens within language. It happens for us, that is, through and as interpretation.

Why can't I go out and "just look" at some object of my experience? I can't because I have always already understood it. Before it comes into view, I am predisposed to see it in a certain way. Let us call this "preunderstanding" to distinguish it from the more deliberate process of understanding as an explicit interpretation. As the following discussion of Heidegger's three-part analysis of preunderstanding shows, it is overwhelmingly implicit and preconscious. It cannot be fully grasped in concepts and statements.

For instance, there is the kind of preunderstanding that comes from immersion in generally social and specifically disciplinary practices, otherwise called, in different contexts, "good breeding," "street sense," "know-how," or "tacit knowledge" (Polanyi 1962, 49–65). Heidegger calls this knowing gained from activity "forehaving"; Thomas Kuhn, thinking more narrowly about the experience a scientist gains from doing science, calls it the "disciplinary matrix"

(Dreyfus 1985, 239). Both formulations involve the impossibility of a pure, disinterested observer of an object world. By insisting on the primacy of practical knowledge over propositional or theoretical knowledge, both invert the valuing of theory over practice commonly encountered in the Western rationalist tradition.

Before we can "have" an object under intellectual scrutiny and control, there is always forehaving. Perhaps this forehaving is clearest in the case of infants, who, as in-fants (without speech), have no propositional knowledge at all. But they "have a world" feelingly, by wandering around in some cultural space and manipulating its objects. We all first "know" the world this way, as, if you will, "pure praxis"—except that this praxis is already impure, because where a child can wander and what she or he can manipulate is prestructured by culture, by, say, a slum tenement rather than a house in the suburbs. Already we can see that preunderstanding is irreducibly social and cultural, "not beliefs . . . but habits and customs embodied in the set of subtle skills which we exhibit in our everyday interaction with things and people" (Dreyfus 1985, 232).

After the advent of language, forehaving is still with us and not only in the sense of all the lookings, feelings, and tastings of infancy. As we say when we are trying to learn a new and difficult practice, we are always more or less "feeling our way along." What this means is that we always "know" before we know: we converse quite capably without knowing anything about turn-taking; we can enter into the world as biology understands it by becoming a biologist, by working within its disciplinary matrix, whether we can say anything about that matrix or not. Our "forehaving," our "situatedness" in social practices common to a culture or some special activity within that culture, does not mean that attempts to understand aspects of the ground plan are without value or that theorizing about disciplinary matrices is a waste of time. Such is not the position of philosophical hermeneutics. To the contrary, never-ending reflection on our forehaving—preunderstanding in the sense of meaning-orientations implicit in our practices—is a significant part of the hermeneutical task. And hermeneutics is theoretical in offering theories of interpretation.

Self-reflection and theory are virtues in philosophical hermeneutics, but they are dependent on praxis. The limitations of *Dasein's* finitude means that reflection cannot bring all "knowing" into knowing and that theory can never be definitive.

The importance of theory for philosophical hermeneutics is clearer in "foresight" and "foreconception," the other two notions in Heidegger's analysis of preunderstanding. Foresight confirms the often-repeated statement that observation itself is theory-laden. What we see is anticipated by "the vocabulary or conceptual scheme we bring to any problem" (Dreyfus 1985, 233). Ancient astronomers saw lights shining in the firmament; we see spheres of light-producing energy, suns more or less like our own, only more distant. Our ancestors saw earthquakes as the hand of God; we see them as sudden slippages along a fault line, understandable as plate tectonics. We retain the notion of "act of God" only as a category for insurance claims.

Foresight is not the imposing of an interpretation on a set of sensations, as if the one were independent of the other. We do not first see something and then attach an interpretation to it. Rather, our conceptual scheme is always "out there," projected ahead of us, so that we are always looking for something and seeing as something. This does not mean that our vocabulary or conceptual scheme determines our sensations. The relationship is not causal in either direction, but concurrent. *Dasein* and interpretations-sensations are inseparable.

The structure of foresight is anticipatory, a matter of expectation, not of causal necessity. Because it is such, our foreseeings may be disappointed, so that we do not observe what we expected to see. We can and do revise our conceptual schemes when what we anticipate fails to appear or does not appear the way we expected; what we cannot do is observe without anticipations, in totally empty neutrality. "Pure seeing" would be the same as not seeing; if we do not *see as,* we do not see at all.

Foresight corresponds to general theory, the overall preunderstanding we have of existence, whether that theory is formal or informal, latent or patent. It is Ptolemy's universe as opposed to Copernicus's; Adam Smith versus Marx. Outside of special fields like cosmology and economics, it is, for example, the belief that "a woman's place is in the home" versus the view that sex-based divisions of labor are outmoded and exploitative. Theory, then, is everywhere, from popular culture to the cultures of specialized disciplines.

Foresight differs from forehaving in being a set of beliefs, in being representable as propositions; forehaving, the ground plan of practices, "does not consist in a belief system, a system of rules, or in formalized procedures, . . . does not consist in representations at all." When we try to represent practices, what we find is "a flexibility which is lost when they are converted into propositional knowledge." Forehaving is the "noncognitive precondition of all understanding" (Dreyfus 1985, 232–33); foreseeing belongs to the cognitive precondition of all understanding.

Foreconception is also cognitive; it consists in "a specific hypothesis which, within the overall theory, can be confirmed or disconfirmed by the data" (Dreyfus 1985, 234). Foreconception predigests our experience of the world. As I do not first have a naked sensation and then try to interpret it, so I do not encounter an anomaly and then grope after a hypothesis to account for it. Rather, I attempt to assimilate all sensations and anomalies to preexisting understandings.

Let us take a commonplace example. I arrive at the office at the usual time to find the outer door locked, not unlocked by the secretary, who always comes to work thirty minutes before my arrival. Even as I fumble for the key I seldom use, I am already filled with hypotheses: "He overslept. He is ill. His car wouldn't start." And so on. I do not think: "He has been abducted by aliens from outer space. Some god has turned him into an oak tree." Although these are possibilities in other frames of preunderstanding, like science fiction and Ovid, they are not the foreconceptions in this context. While I cannot say as yet which of my hypotheses will be confirmed by the data, I already have a finite set of the likely explanations and know what to ask to confirm one of them.

But I will not have to ask. The secretary and I are so *Mitsein* that he will more or less know in advance what I have anticipated and hypothesized. He also knows that social expectations are such that he owes me an explanation, one that falls within the realm of what both of us would take as plausible and acceptable. My foreconceptions, then, are not mine but *Dasein's,* just as my forehaving and foresight are.

Even this brief explication of preunderstanding should reveal its centrality for philosophical hermeneutics. It should be clearer now, for example, exactly what "priority of Being" means. Preunderstanding is precisely what makes the existential notion of Being the always-already-there. It is the before that any conscious understanding is necessarily subsequent to and dependent on. We can understand because we have always already understood; in philosophical hermeneutics the longstanding problem of how a mind can grasp a thing is shown to be what it is: a pseudoproblem. There is no need for bridging the hiatus between minds and things, for there is no hiatus in the first place: both exist for us at their irreducible minimum as implicit meaning. Understanding works with preunderstanding, meaning-making with the already meaningful, the explicit with the implicit—in the language of metaphysics, mind and thing share the same "substance," standing under, or rather standing in language and symbols, the house of Being.

The previous paragraph describes the single best-known formulation of hermeneutics, the hermeneutic circle. Too much has been made of it by both defenders and detractors. For the defenders, it has become sometimes almost a vindication of unreason, a wonderful paradox of nearly mystical dimension. For if we can only understand what we have already understood, if knowing depends on "knowing," then there is no first premise, no necessary beginning point, and therefore the whole edifice of systematic deductive thought is shown to be at best arbitrary and superficial, at worst fraudulent.

The kernel of truth here of course is that, as historical beings, we can set forth only from where we happen to be—our "universal first principles" turn out to be historical after all, like Kant's transcendental time and space, not everybody's time and space, but rather Newton's. But there is nothing illogical about preunderstanding unless one believes that one cannot be logical except by beginning from an undeduced, necessary, or self-evident first premise. Logic itself depends on preunderstanding, the truth of the famous syllogism about Socrates being no more than a formalization, a way of packaging what everybody over the age of ten already knew about humanity and mortality. Likewise, even a pure abstraction, like $a = a$, relies for its cogency on a being whose common experience includes already the postulate of identity, without which we could not cope at all.

For the detractors, the hermeneutical circle has been called vicious in that it allegedly draws the different from the self-same, knowledge from knowledge. But preunderstanding is not the same thing as understanding; reflecting on an interpretation is not the same thing as having one. Others have called attention to the problem of verification. If all we have is interpretations of reality, or worse, interpretations of interpretations of interpretations *ad infinitum,* in what can any assertion rest? How can we assess the truth claim implicit in any interpretation? The fear is that the hermeneutical circle leaves us in an "anything goes" situation, a complete and chaotic relativism.

Does it? What exactly is truth for philosophical hermeneutics? How do we know when we have it or when it has us?

Truth as Disclosure

To the question "What is truth?" philosophical hermeneutics replies that "Being itself is an event of truth" (Gadamer 1976b, 224). But what does this mean?

Before *Dasein*, before human-being-in-the-world, there was no tradition or culture carried by symbols and language within which beings could appear. We may assume that natural events occurred, as they would still occur if *Dasein* exits from existence, but no events of truth occurred because there was no being to care and to question, no truth-seeker.

In the first place, then, truth is always truth *for someone*. The common sense notion that truth simply is somehow, independent of us, and that we discover it in the same way that Columbus bumped into America while attempting a western passage to India deprives truth of its history, its coming-to-be. In one sense of the word *relative*, truth is relative, for it requires a relation to *Dasein*, to time and place. Truth is historical.

To say, however, that truth is always truth for someone, to say that truth is historical, is not to say that anything goes. We will see why in a later section called "Dialogue, Dialectic, and the Fusion of Horizons."

The advent of *Dasein* is the advent of Being and beings, since we cannot imagine human being without culture, language, and tradition. To speak casually of the advent of Being and beings is in one way quite misleading. For it implies a sudden emergence into simple presence, as in the momentary transition between not being conscious of something and becoming aware of it. Being and beings never have a simple presence for *Dasein*. Both exist in concealment, in hiddenness. As the clearing in which beings appear, Being hides itself in beings; we attend, that is, to the matter at hand, whatever happens to be the subject of our thought and speech at any one moment, not to the flow of preexisting meaning within which everything comes to mind or to language. As language is normally transparent to us, so is Being. It requires quite an effort to recall its "being there" always ahead of us. Such is our finitude that we cannot think about Being and beings simultaneously, any more than we can, at the same time, attend to linguistic forms and what is being said through them.

Not only are we always more or less forgetting Being, but beings also withhold themselves. In thinking about some something now, what usually escapes us is that, as Gadamer says, "the most primordial mode in which the past is present is not remembering, but forgetting" (1976b, 203). Behind our individual sense of identity, of self-possession, there is everything that has formed us; even the most conscientious autobiography is an incomplete remembrance of things past. After Freud, no one can doubt that our individual past is mostly a forgetting, recollected only partially and painfully.

As the self is mostly a forgetting, so also is the human-made, cultural environment in which we move about. Here the past has a presence as solid as the building in which we work. But what do we know of this building whose spaces we inhabit mostly without a thought of its interpretational history or what it represents? Who wanted it built and why? What was the architect's idea and inspiration? How faithfully was the idea translated into wood and steel and bricks and mortar? What does it "say" now, in a different environment, surrounded by other buildings of later vintage? And so on. There is no end to the questions we could ask or to filling out the answers.

If our second nature is mostly opaque to us, what is the condition of our understanding of natural objects and life-forms, whose coming into being was not by our hands? We are justly proud of how much more we know about the history of the earth and the evolution of life than was known only a generation ago, but the thoughtful natural scientist knows how little this "how much more" really is. The geological record preserves just enough to tantalize, bits and pieces of a mostly missing puzzle made into a whole as an always-about-to-be-torn tissue of speculation, which is to say, interpretation.

As the ancient skeptic observed, truth is "in the depths," covered over by the earth, eroded by time, lost in the forgetfulness of *Dasein's* unreflective living in the world. What little is present to our severely limited awareness exists only by virtue of absence, by that which cannot be accessed for one reason or another and by that which is recalled only partially and held together with much effort.

Absence, then, for philosophical hermeneutics is a more embracing notion than Derrida's semiological "trace." It takes in not only our "forgetting" of the system of language, whose implicit contrasts (of phonemes, for instance) enables the explicit meanings of discourse, but also any sense in which the past is forgotten in the present. More than that, because "time has its being not in the 'now' or the succession of nows, but rather in the essentially futural character of *Dasein*" (Gadamer 1976b, 204)—because we exist in thrownness but as projection, in anticipation and expectation—we live always amid the not-yet, in absence.

Being's primordial and continuing presence is absence: Being and beings exist in concealment or hiddenness. It follows, therefore, that before truth can be anything else, it has to be truth in the root sense of the Greek word for truth, *a-letheia*, an unforgetting, unhiddenness, disclosure. Somehow beings reveal themselves in the light or clearing of Being. But how exactly?

Horizon and Prejudice

Thus far we have said that truth for philosophical hermeneutics is always truth for *Dasein,* human being in some time and place. Truth is historical. Put another way, philosophical hermeneutics entertains a situational or contextual theory of truth, as opposed to the dominant Western theory of truth as universal and objective.

Instead of situation or context, philosophical hermeneutics commonly uses Husserl's term "horizon" (Gadamer 1976b, 188–89). All three words share implications that can seriously mislead. They imply a "just-thereness," whereas they are interpretations, implicitly as preunderstanding (forehaving, foreseeing, and foreconception), explicitly as understanding, assertions about the world. The three words also imply fixity, whereas our being in the world is emergent, immanent, dynamic. Horizon has the further liability of being a visual metaphor, whereas philosophical hermeneutics tends to think of truth more as something we "listen for" rather than "look at." At least horizon has some implications more in keeping with the notion of Being as a truth-event. For instance, horizon is projective, unfolding ahead of us as our preunderstandings and understandings do, altering as our location alters, rather than being static like the metaphor of a framework. If we hold on to the temporal implications of horizon, it will do.

So understood, horizon is indispensable to philosophical hermeneutics because truth as unhiddenness designates the coming-to-presence of things and events as meanings anticipated within a horizon of projected meanings. When, for example, the Berlin Wall began to come down, no one saw only the dismantling of so much steel and concrete. What we saw was what our predisposition toward meaning allowed us to see: the liberation of Eastern Europe; the inevitable triumph of the human desire to be free; the triumph of democracy and free enterprise over totalitarianism and Communism. And so on. These interpretations, seemingly after the fact, actually preexisted the first piece removed by chisel and hammer from the wall itself. They are not interpretations concocted after the fact to account for "raw data." Rather, the event called forth understandings deeply rooted in preunderstandings, in the practices, general theories, and specific hypotheses of the Western democracies or the "free world," itself an interpretation.

If we grant that truth first manifests itself as unhiddenness—and we can hardly conclude otherwise if we accept *Dasein's* being as thrown-projection—then we must also recognize the positive role of prejudice in bringing about truth. We have been taught that prejudice can only be a barrier to truth, that we should want to shed our prejudice and be objective. Truth is the opposite of prejudice.

Against this Enlightenment view of truth, Gadamer points out that "the historicity of our existence entails that prejudices, in the literal sense of the word [that is, prejudgments], constitute the initial directness of our whole ability to experience. Prejudices are biases of our openness to the world." If we do not see as, we do not see at all; to understand is to exist already in preunderstandings. A horizon is a set of prejudgments, prejudices in the root sense of the word. We could have no experience at all without them. We are what we are because of them: "It is not so much our judgments as it is our prejudgments that constitute our being" (1976b, 9).

Our prejudgments alter, but we are never without them: it is "the fact of prejudices as such, and not of one permanent, inflexible set of them" (Linge 1976, xviii) that is characteristic of *Dasein's* being in time. Insofar as we have evolved elaborate methodologies designed to do the impossible, to set aside bias, to pretend that we have no preunderstanding of our subject of inquiry, we have wasted much effort in the cause of self-deceit.

And what does devotion to method most conceal from us? Our being in time, our immersion in the authority of traditions. For where does any prejudice come from? Clearly, only from the collective revelation of the past, from books, from tales told over and over, works of art, social and disciplinary practices, old buildings that we live in, still older buildings whose ruins and associated artifacts we study. The prejudice against prejudice is also a prejudice against tradition, a tendency to equate authority with falsehood, as if anything that manages to survive from the past has to be the source of error, ignorance, and superstition. But as some prejudices are enabling and some are disabling, so the past's authority is not something we can either celebrate uncritically or condemn wholesale as human bondage. The choice is not all or nothing; it is much harder than that. We must detect somehow the right prejudices for our place and time, the ones that allow our truths to emerge with the least distortion, distinguish somehow between traditions worth preserving and those no longer helpful, and offer our allegiance to authorities that actually merit it.

Somehow. Truth first appears to us within horizons, as the coming-to-presence of meanings anticipated by our prejudices. But the hermeneutical task has only begun. The rest of the work is reflection, exposure of and inquiry into preunderstanding itself. Truth as unhiddenness allows us to see something amid the flux of happenings, but the human imperative is Kent's urgent appeal to King Lear to "see better." Hermeneutical reflection must reflect on something, so that truth as disclosure is always first. The latter's truth, however, must undergo the trials of experience and dialogue to become something more than the thoughtless repetition of an inheritance. Truth as unhiddenness, therefore, is ultimately no less dependent on reflection than reflection is on unhiddenness. They are moments in the dialectic of truth's revealing-concealing of itself.

Dialogue, Dialectic, and the Fusion of Horizons

> Opposition is true friendship.
>
> —William Blake

Just the mention of truth and dialectic together is enough to recall Plato and Hegel, the origin and the culmination of metaphysics, respectively—or so Kirkegaard, Nietzsche, and Heidegger have taught us. But have we not said already that philosophical hermeneutics fashions itself around a critique of the metaphysics of presence and the epistemology of subject and object? What exactly is going on? Do the implications of truth as *aletheia* amount to letting metaphysics in by the back door?

Heidegger seems to have thought so; in his later philosophy he tried to move beyond the focus in *Being and Time* (1962) on *Dasein's* horizons, which he came to see as too close to subjectivism and humanism's tendency to make human being the measure of all things (1977a, 202–211). And Derrida finds the metaphysics of presence in both early and late Heidegger as well as philosophical hermeneutics generally.

We can appreciate Heidegger's capacity for radical rethinking of his own project and Derrida's insights into what he called "the metaphorics of Being's proximity" (1987, 146) in Heidegger without concluding that philosophical hermeneutics simply brings Plato and Hegel back as the metaphysics of presence. Actually philosophical hermeneutics, especially as Gadamer develops it, "retrieves" Plato and Hegel in the sense of retrieval in Heidegger, that is, reinterpreting them within the concerns of contemporary thought, which means both listening to what they have to say to us now and letting what no longer connects drop away. In other words, the "return" to Plato and Hegel is a thoughtful return that both preserves and destroys. *It is precisely the difference between retrieval and deconstruction that separates Gadamer from Derrida.*

Both Gadamer and Derrida are postmodern, if in using that term we mean a philosophy no longer foundational in intent, no longer metaphysics or epistemology in the modernist way of Descartes. Separating philosophical hermeneutics from Descartes and from the very different foundationalisms of Plato and Hegel is, above all else, *Dasein's* temporality, its radical finitude. As thrown-projection, *Dasein* can lay no claim to truth in the sense of a beginning point secure from doubt or revision, as in Descartes; nor to a recollection of an ultimate and absolute origin before or beyond history, as in Plato; nor to a Christian-Hegelian revelation of the endtime, history's fruition in total understanding. As a historical being, *Dasein* is thrown into the middle of things, into a past that stretches back into—What? Who knows?— and stretches out toward the future as plans and projects, but towards ultimately another unknown. All *Dasein* knows for certain is death; in moments of authenticity, we care and question within the urgency of finiteness, in "fear and trembling."

As long as philosophical hermeneutics holds fast to its existential ontology of *Dasein,* it cannot be fairly accused of a secret hankering after metaphysics or epistemology. As long as it does not forget that *Dasein* is *Mitsein,* that human-being-in-the-world is being-with-others, it cannot be fairly accused of falling into subjectivism. For *Dasein* is a collective inheritance, an ongoing dialogue of many voices, not a harmonious chorus with one message, as we tend to think when we use a word like tradition. Nor is *Dasein* humanistic in the sense of elevating human being over all existence. Human being is the measure of all things only in the sense that it is the being that measures. But its ways of sizing up have no ultimate or absolute warrant or justification. Rather, we understand according to our preunderstandings, by standards that are social and cultural, not metaphysical.

What, then, can philosophical hermeneutics find in Plato and Hegel worth retrieving? From Plato it takes dialogue as the hermeneutical mode of inquiry; from Hegel, a dialectical understanding of truth as permanently tensive, a revealing that conceals, a bringing to presence amid absence. Let us take a closer look at both.

If *Dasein's* being is finitude—if it cannot have "the whole truth and nothing but the truth"—and if *Dasein* is *Mitsein* in its being a being-with-others, then the preconditions for and the impetus toward dialogue are always latent in human existence, even when it is manifestly absent, when it is repressed or suppressed. We are a dialogue that needs dialogue. We no more choose it than we choose to breathe or to acquire our first language.

But the self-conscious opting for dialogue as the hermeneutical mode of inquiry is quite a different matter, one that cannot be justified simply by appeal to *Dasein's* ontology. Why, for instance, should we want to engage in a dialogue with a text rather than analyze it? Why treat a text as something that speaks rather than as an object?

We established earlier that philosophical hermeneutics develops from a critique of subject-object thinking. Mind and thing, human being and beings dwell together in language, the house of Being, before they are sundered into subjects and objects by epistemology. The artificial and abstract separation of consciousness from what it is conscious of is exactly what philosophical hermeneutics would overcome with its stressing of preunderstanding, interpretation, and truth as unhiddenness. But method as it has been generally understood since Descartes begins by assuming the subject-object dichotomy, its function being primarily to bracket subjective prejudices and to push the lived-with things of our life-world out to arm's length where they can be safely observed without involvement. Such is "the way," the method of objectivity, the positivism of scientific inquiry and its technical applications.

Philosophical hermeneutics throws into fundamental question the whole idea of method as a privileged access to truth. But what does it offer in its stead? The answer is dialogue, which, when the dialogue is genuine, does not work within a subject-object framework. What justifies this claim?

There are no objects in dialogue, but rather the matter under discussion, the issue, theme, or question. Dialogue may appeal to the common experience of the interlocutors, but its business is not observation. Dialogue is not a thing or object-oriented affair.

There are also no subjects in dialogue, but rather participants. On the one hand, in sharp contrast to the methods of objectivism, dialogue admits and even welcomes personalities and strongly held opinions. Instead of attempting to bracket or exclude the prejudices erroneously identified with "mere subjectivity," dialogue proposes to work with and through personalities and opinions. On the other hand, to the extent that interaction remains a clash of personalities or only an exchange of opinion, dialogue has not yet begun.

Dialogue is not eristic. The point of it is not to hold a position against all challengers, but to listen, to allow one's opinions to be matured by opening oneself to partners in the dialogue whose horizons differ from our own. In a genuine dialogue, as Gadamer says, "something different comes to be" (1976b, 58). And where does it come to be? *Not "in me" or "in you," but rather "in the between," via the exchange itself,* as we work from some degree of shared preunderstandings (or we could not converse at all) and towards intersubjective understanding and, when possible, agreement. In genuine dialogue carried along by the dynamics of the exchange, we lose ourselves in the matter at hand, subjectivity disappears into participation.

Dialogue is the way of hermeneutics insofar as it is nonmethodical. Hermeneutics has its methodical side; interpretation of older texts especially requires historical linguistics or philology, as integral to understanding as method is to empirical investigation. But method is not designed to inquire into preunderstanding; method belongs to the horizon of subject-object thinking and cannot, as method, challenge subject-object thinking.

Horizons are challenged in ways too hit-or-miss to be called methodical—when events do not answer to our anticipations, when actions based on an interpretation of events prove inadequate, when we are open to dialogue. Method knows how to proceed, what to do to assure that its conclusions can be replicated; dialogue must find what to say and what to ask in the midst of the dialogue itself, which cannot be replicated.

To return to the question of truth in hermeneutics: how, then, can dialogue contribute anything to truth? In dialogue we can sometimes achieve what Gadamer calls a "fusion of horizons" (1989b, 273–74), an event of truth, a revealing-concealing that goes beyond the spontaneous, unscrutinized projections of preunderstanding. In this fusion of horizons, we return to Hegel's dialectic, but with a crucial difference.

The motto of philosophical hermeneutics could well be "truth keeps happening" (Weinsheimer 1985, 9), another way of saying that Being is an event of truth. People, things, events—in short, our world—come to presence as the prejudged, the always already understood or interpreted. This is truth for us, and no less truth when we become aware that truth is inseparable from bias. We still "see" (perceive, understand) the same world. What can alter us is genuine dialogue with "the other," which means risking the very prejudices that make our world and constitute our truths. Dialogue moves in two directions: "back" towards our preunderstandings, for nothing exposes them better for us than dialogue with someone whose prejudices do not merely reinforce our own—in such moments of grace, we in fact first become aware of our biases as biases—and "forward" toward achieving a common understanding, toward agreement, or at least toward recognition of exactly what we disagree about and why. This forward movement, though it cannot occur without the movement back as well, is what Gadamer means by fusion of horizons. It designates the will to truth peculiar to dialogue, the back and forth of discussion as we struggle toward consensus, a new sharing of truth, though still truth for us, historical and contextual, and even if resolution is achieved, still tentative and temporary, open to the next opportunity for dialogue.

What, then, is truth for philosophical hermeneutics? It happens in "the between," among us, as we attempt to enlarge our horizons by incorporating the insights of the other, even as the other is challenged by what we ask and assert. Truth is whatever emerges from the dialogue, wherever we come to rest this time.

Does truth as never-ending inquiry leave us in an anything-goes situation? Hardly. In the first place, the spontaneous, unexamined truths disclosed by our horizons have their origin in traditions with definite content. Not just anything comes to unconcealment, but only what our prejudices allow us to see. Far from anything goes, the biases of our openness to the world are normally too selective. Not enough goes. Dogmatic closure is a constant threat to *Dasein's* authenticity.

In the second place, the openings up of dialogue scarcely amount to anything goes. As a process of unconcealment itself, a violent process that alters all participants, that challenges our very being, dialogue permits to stand only what can withstand the encounter. There is no method for this finding and no assurances that what we discover between us will be sufficient. But at least what two or more minds find compelling is likely to be less insufficient. In our finitude we cannot see totally, but sometimes we can see better, learning to distinguish the true daughter from the false ones without having to lose everything first.

"The learned is the suffered." The question is: Will the sufferance be by dialogue or by tragedy? We can rest assured in any case that Being's truth event is not equivalent to anything goes.

Finally, why should we want to dialogue with a text rather than— or at least more than—analyze it? Treated as an object, textual otherness loses its transforming power, its claim to truth. It becomes something for us to operate on, something never allowed to operate on us. "But a text can begin to speak" (Gadamer 1976b, 57) and must be allowed to speak, not because it should have an unquestioned authority, as canonical texts do for some people, but because its authority poses a question for us, namely: What does it say to us now? If it says nothing, it is dead, canonical or not. But until we have listened for its truths, we have not earned the privilege of calling it dead, just as we have not earned the privilege of deconstructing a living text until we have permitted it to question our own horizons. The potential for unmaking-remaking must extend in both directions, from the interpreter to the text and from the text to the interpreter, or we have fallen out of the dialogue, opting either for text idolatry or a mere pretense to superiority.

And what of Hegel's dialectic? How does philosophical hermeneutics retrieve it within a commitment to dialogue? On the de-structive side of retrieval, the key phrase is "within a commitment to dialogue." Hegel had no such commitment, conceiving his dialectic as a kind of internal monologue, whose progression from one concept to another was necessary and whose inevitable end was totality, the whole, Absolute Spirit. The drama of dialogue is an interaction of persons, not of concepts, and therefore unpredictable and never total. All that is metaphysical and methodical in Hegel drops away.

On the constructive side of retrieval, philosophical hermeneutics preserves Hegel's highly developed awareness of truth as an event, as history, something that reveals itself in time, that is tensive and unstable, dynamic in its incompleteness, always "on the way." The key phrase here is "fusion of horizons," a near relation to Hegel's *Aufhebung,* which designates a process of cancelling, preserving, and moving beyond, all more or less simultaneously. *Aufhebung* describes well what happens in genuine dialogue, when something different comes to be. Our initial stances are negated or cancelled. The other helps us to see our partiality, the blindness of our insights. At the same time, each participant has something to offer to the common understanding that we are attempting to fashion via the give-and-take of dialogue itself. Whatever we bring to the encounter that stands up to scrutiny must find a place in the new truths emerging. And whatever does emerge in this cancelling-preserving is obviously a moving beyond where we were when the conversation began. Our horizons do not fuse in the sense of complete identity; if I become the other, I lose the other's friendly opposition, which prevents me from becoming too hopelessly myself. Rather, our horizons fuse in the sense of a mutual enlargement of horizons, which still remain different.

No amount of dialogue, however, can overcome the hiddenness of truth, the absence in whatever is present for us. As Gadamer remarks, "Reflection on a given preunderstanding brings before me something that otherwise happens behind my back. Something—but not everything . . . [for consciousness, *Bewusstsein*] is inescapably more being [*Sein*] than consciousness [*Bewusst*]" (1976b, 38). We are always more than we know or can know. Truth remains always an endless process of unforgetting and therefore "an opposition of revealment and concealment" (226). It is this opposition, the dialectical tensiveness of truth, that drives the dialogue on.

The Experienced Person and Practical Judgment

What is the end or function of philosophical hermeneutics? This is the question that the last of our *topoi* answers.

We have been concerned with the meaning of truth for philosophical hermeneutics, but we cannot say that its end is truth. Foundational philosophy or metaphysics can and did make such a claim for itself, but philosophical hermeneutics cannot. If Being is an event of truth, truth cannot be the special end of any one discipline. If truth is always present-absent, a revealing that conceals, no one can claim to have it.

Philosophical hermeneutics does claim to understand understanding itself, the truth process. But to call that its end would be to confuse its focus of concern, its theme or subject matter, with an end or function.

Philosophical hermeneutics shares with Mikhail Bakhtin, Martin Buber, Richard Rorty, and others a desire to keep the conversation going, a certain faith in the value of genuine dialogue. Here is a commitment that has some power to set philosophical hermeneutics and kindred ways of doing philosophy apart from other modes of inquiry and other ways of doing philosophy. Dialogue is the choice of natural over artificial languages, an opting for the unpredictable process of question and answer over method; for the examined life, inquiry into prejudice, over a concern with, say, formal systems or objectivized processes.

But while the cultivation of dialogue has some power to distinguish, it hardly distinguishes enough. So much contemporary thought converges in a renewal of dialogue that one could almost call dialogue the *telos* (end) of our time. If we ask, "What sort of awareness or attitude lends itself to genuine dialogue?" we can, in taking an answer from philosophical hermeneutics, also come nearer to its end or function.

The person disposed toward dialogue and who can best profit from and contribute to such an exchange has cultivated what Gadamer calls "consciousness of effective history" (1976b, 27-28). This means that the person is aware not only of prejudices as such, but of the situatedness of one's own prejudices, the fact that one's own assumptions, beliefs, attitudes—everything brought to a dialogue—belongs to a (not "the") tradition. The key term is "effective": history is not so much understanding what happened back then, but understanding its continuing impact on us now. Such an understanding implies an awareness of the contingency of even our most cherished beliefs, which means a certain capacity for overcoming a blinding investment of ego in them. We still hold what we hold, but in openness, not as something dropped from the sky inscribed by God's own hand. In contrast, the "natural attitude," the common stance of most people most of the time, is that all right-thinking people share or ought to share our position. Such a stance is one of the many forces at work that sabotages dialogue, which turns an opportunity for increasing self-understanding into merely an exchange of opinion.

If our ontological condition is thrownness, that thrownness does not imply any necessary awareness of thrownness per se or of the effective history of its contents. "Consciousness of effective history" must be cultivated; it is the end or function of hermeneutical education to bring to awareness and thus to the possibility of critique as much of our effective history as possible. This end distinguishes it from education as monologue, knowledge about something and training to method or technique. Neither as such requires reflexive self-application. Consciousness of effective history also sets hermeneutical education apart from its own tradition, Socratic dialogue, which examines the internal coherence of opinions without much explicit attention to their context in differing traditions. Hermeneutical education, that is, depends upon the relatively recent development of a sense of history.

Another way to express the aim of philosophical hermeneutics is to say that its goal is the "experienced person" (Gadamer 1989b, 355). No discipline, of course, has experience as its province; experience, in fact, is precisely what eludes knowledge, method, training, and effective history itself. "Experience is initially always experience of negation" (354). That is, we "have an experience" most acutely when our horizons prove inadequate, when we are disappointed, when matters fail to turn out as we anticipated. Experience "just happens," not to all alike, but to all.

Philosophical hermeneutics has two roles to play in the never-completed cultivation of the experienced person. First, it insists on the value of a particular kind of experience, dialogue, where perhaps all experience is most readily shared. The readiness to enter into genuine dialogue characterizes the experienced person, while dialogue itself edifies, helping the experienced person to build and rebuild himself or herself. Second, philosophical hermeneutics fosters a particular attitude toward "the other," and nothing is more "other" than the intrusive negativity of experience. For the dogmatic person, "the other" is something or someone to ignore, refute, or dismiss, an anomaly or irrelevancy. Experience is lost on such a person, who remains in the richest of environments an inexperienced person. The openness of hermeneutical dialogue not only lends itself to having experiences, but also to doing something with them. The other must be allowed to speak in hermeneutical dialogue—that is its great imperative—which means that, rather than suppressing or thrusting aside what does not conform to our prejudgments, we allow the negativity of experience to alter prejudice itself. In this way we gain experience rather than waste it; in this way we turn the negative into a positive.

Consciousness of effective history and the experienced person are ends in themselves inasmuch as civility is a virtue and civilization a good. For the dogmatic person is the uncivil person, unfit for the business of any community. And yet consciousness of effective history and the experienced person are also only preparatory for something else, what the Greeks called *phronesis*, practical judgment, the ability to choose the right course or to do the right thing amid the contingencies of daily life, when mechanical applications of rules are not sufficient.

Phronesis is ethics in action; amid conflicting imperatives and the circumstances of a particular case, the individual or group responsible for making a decision must discover the best course of action. Such is the role, for example, of judge or jury in legal cases, of the family when the life of one of its members is being sustained by artificial means, of institutional officials unable to handle a request in the usual ways, of parents who must resolve conflicts between themselves or among their children in ways acceptable to all concerned. *Phronesis* is obviously hermeneutical through and through: the general principles or rules relevant to the case at hand must be interpreted and, in instances of conflicting principles, interpreted in the sense of rank-ordered. The particular instance itself must be interpreted in the sense of a summational judgment of its quality, especially its motives. And principles and instance must "come together," interpreted in the sense of adjusting norms to circumstances in the interest of justice or fairness.

Clearly no algorithm can be applied where practical judgment must be exercised; that is why we can speak of an art of living, a talent or a knack for doing the right thing. Just as clearly, the openness of the experienced person is a precondition of *phronesis*, because self-reflection on the limitations of one's own prejudices and careful heeding of the dialogue of "the old" (of precedent in the widest sense) and of "the new" (the "facts" in this case) are exactly what is required.

In short, then, hermeneutical education cultivates the experienced person, the person best prepared for the complexities of practical judgment, for the exercise of a responsible and ethical authority.

———————

Apart from the next chapter, the rest of this book amounts to an exploratory sketching of a hermeneutical rhetoric.

But before moving on to hermeneutical rhetoric, we need to ask one more question: Why choose philosophical hermeneutics as a general intellectual stance? Why not instead some form of negative hermeneutics, like neo-Marxism? Why not deconstruction, which, at least as Derrida develops it, subverts both philosophical and negative hermeneutics? Some of the issues in choosing and the significance of the choice are the next concern.

4 Why Philosophical Hermeneutics?

With the title of this chapter, we return to the question from which we set out, but with a difference in focus: in chapter one, I explained the significance of philosophical hermeneutics within hermeneutics generally; here I want to concentrate on the stake rhetoricians have in its categories and attitudes. More specifically, I want to show why a rhetorician should prefer the stance of philosophical over negative hermeneutics, especially as deconstruction.

One need only read Brian Vickers's *Defence of Rhetoric* (1988) to be reminded how hostile philosophy has been to rhetoric. Since Plato, with very few exceptions, philosophy has held that rhetoric is an empty and vain art, an art for deceivers and charlatans; or that it is no art at all, but a mere knack, like cooking or cosmetics; or that—and here we reach the limit of philosophical charity—a technique that might be useful as a way of popularizing the truths that only dialectic or only science or only revealed religion can establish.

What we are witnessing is the revenge of rhetoric. Its roots extend back at least to Kierkegaard, who was, among the major figures of modern philosophy, the first and still one of the best puncturers of philosophical inflation. Then there was Nietzsche, who actually bothered to study rhetoric and to lecture about it. He showed us that philosophical discourse is rhetoric, that its pretension to have something beyond "mere persuasion" is actually mere pretense. He showed us also that philosophy hates rhetoric because it hates the flux, the ever-changing climate of opinion and ever-different exigencies that rhetoric strives modestly to cope with, rather than, like foundational philosophy, to displace with "the Truth." And now there is Derrida who, at least as I understand him, has finished the job Nietzsche began.

Any rhetorician aware of the contempt that philosophy has had for rhetoric cannot fail to take delight in deconstruction. True enough, we can complain about the tendency of Derrida and his followers to reduce rhetoric to style, but that tendency is at least as old as Gorgias and typical of literary rhetoricians from Longinus to Paul de Man. What counts most for us, and probably accounts for much of the appeal Derrida has among rhetoricians, is that deconstruction makes undecidables out of philosophical verities and enlarges the realm of rhetoric, the uncertain and the disputable. Except as a commonplace, anything reified into Truth is lost to rhetoric; undoing reifications is one of Derrida's special talents. What more could a rhetorician ask of an influential reader of philosophical texts?

Why not follow the lead of Jasper Neel in *Plato, Derrida, and Writing* (1988), Sharon Crowley, and others in seeking—carefully and critically—to ally rhetoric with deconstruction?

I have two objections primarily. From Richard Young, Alton Becker, and Kenneth Pike's *Rhetoric: Discovery and Change* on, "new rhetoric" for teachers of composition has inclined toward discussion. Derrida shows us how to awaken anyone who has fallen into dogmatic slumbers, how to provoke the self-convinced in a way that might lead to dialogue. But can a deconstructionist play that role and enter into dialogue in good faith? Does deconstruction lend itself to a discussion rhetoric?

Right next to dogmatic slumber itself, nothing is more inimical to dialogue than playing what Gadamer calls the role of "spoil sport," the person who thinks she or he has "seen through" what we are saying to our "real motives," our "hidden agenda" (1976b, 41–42). In an age of negative hermeneutics, surely everyone knows about Gadamer's spoil sport. We offer good reasons for holding a position and wait for our partner in the dialogue to either agree or show us where our thinking went wrong, what our point of view omits, or why our good reasons are not so good. What we get instead is a question-begging, wholesale dismissal of our argument as the metaphysics of presence, or ideology, or mere rationalization of deeper, unconscious fears and desires, or covert sexism, or whatever—something that implies that our interlocutor need not take our argument seriously as an argument. Quite rightly we resent this move, and our resentment results in breaking off the exchange or in the degeneration of dialogue into eristic.

Derrida-inspired interpretation tends to spoil dialogue in two ways. First, like Marxism and Freudianism and all their neo-variants, it grinds a single ax to razor sharpness—in the case of deconstruction, the ax with which it hopes to lop off the metaphysics of presence. It strains after the signs of metaphysics with the same obsessive intensity that a Marxist looks for class conflict or a Freudian for the Oedipal conflict. This is not the stance of openness, not the attitude that allows the other to speak.

Second, unlike interpretation inspired by Marx or Freud, Derridean interpretation, when it is close to Derrida's own tactics, makes no affirmations of its own. In attacking Being, Derrida does not advance nihilism; he has no message of his own to impart, but, as John D. Caputo remarks, aims to put Hermes out of work (1987, 160). The idea, as old as some of the ancient skeptics, is to suspend affirming, to not make truth claims at all. Without truth claims, obviously there is nothing to discuss.

Derrida is an extremely attentive reader. There is much to learn from him, much that we can use against antirhetorical philosophy. Deconstruction is a powerful tool, but an occasional tool, not a way of reading that a rhetorician committed to genuine dialogue will want to use often.

My second objection to Derrida is closely related to the first, because how one receives tradition has everything to do with how one interacts with it. The general stance toward tradition that one finds in philosophical hermeneutics is a tensive closeness. Whatever is vital in tradition for us, whatever past voices speak to us now, our relationship to it and them is irremediably ambivalent. We are close to our tradition inasmuch as we have internalized it, made it a part of our identity or being-in-the-world. But insofar as a text was addressed to a situation that no longer exists, we also are tension-filled, driven to reread the text in our different context. Without some degree of proximity to the other, dialogue is difficult and seldom fruitful; without tensions, the other has appropriated us, rather than we it, and there is nothing to talk about. Retrieval is motivated by a nearness that is also, simultaneously, a distance.

Derrida's attitude toward tradition is revealed best in one of his critiques of Heidegger (1987). In accord with the hermeneutical stance toward the past, Heidegger aimed to get beyond metaphysics by working through metaphysics, by remaining in dialogue with the other, much as Plato depicts Socrates in dialogue with his other, Protagoras, Gorgias, and other representatives of Sophism. Derrida, however, while recognizing the impossibility of a definitive break with the past, nevertheless clearly favors "a change of terrain" (151). He seems to hold that, as long as Heidegger remained in conversation with the metaphysical tradition, he remained a captive of it. What we must do, Derrida's metaphor implies, is take up ground outside our philosophical heritage and presumably build anew.

Here Derrida reveals his own tradition, for the way he advocates is the way of Descartes and amounts to a kind of inverted Cartesianism. Descartes wanted to start over, to jettison what he perceived as the dead weight of Scholasticism. Derrida wants to do the same with the metaphysics of presence. True, Descartes wanted to find an indubitable first, whereas Derrida denies the firstness of firsts, whether as privileged origins in the past or as axioms for a deductive thought system. Hence, inverted Cartesianism—as resolute in its pursuit of undecidability as Descartes was in trying to find something that even his profound skepticism could not doubt. But the move with respect to tradition is much the same.

Inverted or not, Cartesianism is hardly rhetoric's friend. Like dialogue, rhetoric functions best when writer and reader are in tension-filled proximity. Without proximity, in the absence of shared preunderstandings and interpretations, the rhetor has no persuasive resources, nothing with which to effect the reader's identification. But without tensions, there would of course be no rhetorical situation. As Kenneth Burke remarks, under conditions of pure difference and pure identity, rhetoric has no function; in the former it is impossible, in the latter unnecessary or only ceremonial (1969b, 25). Derrida's *différance*, his emphasis on undermining identification, either by stressing *différance* or by endless deferral of both assent and dissent, moves toward making rhetoric impossible. His focus on dissemination is an effort to disperse persuasive force, to deprive it of the very presence that, as Chaim Perelman points out, it is rhetoric's primary task to create (1969, 116–17). In short, deconstruction works against both rhetoric and dialogue by a one-sided stressing of the absence in presence.

"One-sided" is the key to understanding why deconstruction—or for that matter any type of negative hermeneutics—cannot fully serve our turn. Rhetoric, as Aristotle said, "proves opposites" (1932, 6); that is, the skilled rhetor can find the available means of persuasion on both or all sides of an issue. The rhetor knows in advance that there is usually something to say for all parties in a dispute, that the right decision can emerge only through open conflict under controlled conditions of exchange—in a court of law, say, or a congress of delegates or representatives. For the rhetorician the problem with negative hermeneutics is not so much a question of whether Marx, Freud, or Derrida is right or wrong in any particular interpretation, but rather that a primary commitment to any of them amounts to an overcommitment. The rhetorician has faith in the process of open conflict itself, not in Marx, Freud, or Derrida.

The rhetorician's task is not to grind one ax, but to help people sharpen whatever ax they are grinding, the object being an improvement in the quality of exchange generally, whether that exchange is the question and answer of dialogue or the monologues of advocacy.

Is Gadamer's philosophical hermeneutics likewise one-sided?

Yes, as all projects of finite human beings are. Its source is the Romantic reaction against the Enlightenment's antitraditional stance. It is the Enlightenment's faith in method that philosophical hermeneutics counters with faith in dialogue. Philosophical hermeneutics has an agenda as surely as Marxism or deconstruction does. It is not, like poetics, rhetoric, and hermeneutics as text interpretation, a *techne,* an art whose end is to produce something, a work of literature, a discourse, an interpretation. Rather, like Marxism or deconstruction, it has a more definite character and an ethics, a way of being in the world.

Why, then, should a rhetorician adopt its *ethos* over negative hermeneutics?

Rhetorical art is governed by exigency, by what is fitting or appropriate to a situation as the rhetor understands (that is, interprets) it. Sometimes unmasking or deconstructing of the position of one's opponent is unavoidable and even helpful. But it is dangerous business. Of all people, it is the professional rhetorician who should know that everyone is wearing a mask, that everyone's constructions are vulnerable. Thrust will be answered by counterthrust, the unmasker will be unmasked, the deconstructor deconstructed. When the game is played this way, nobody's house avoids the torch. Negative hermeneutics lacks the charity toward the other that philosophical hermeneutics embodies. Rhetoricians want to ply the art, to have their argument taken seriously as an argument. Normally, therefore, they will want to display the charity toward the opponent that they hope the opponent will return in kind. Civilized exchange depends on charity; nonviolent resolution of conflict depends on civilized exchange. The *ethos* of philosophical hermeneutics is implicit in rhetoric, which aims "to convince and illuminate without being able to prove," to recall Gadamer's words.

If, in sum, rhetoric needs a theory of interpretation—and surely because it works with nothing but interpretations, it needs a theory to approach a fuller understanding of itself—that theory should come mainly from philosophical hermeneutics. If a discussion rhetoric is what we are after, a dialogical hermeneutics is its complement. Our goal should be dialogue with all the voices of negative hermeneutics, not the adopting of one of its voices as a guiding light. Richard Bernstein remarks near the end of a lengthy critique of *Truth and Method* that "what Gadamer is appealing to is a concept of truth that comes down to what can be argumentatively validated by the community of interpreters who open themselves to what is 'handed down' ... to us" (1986, 99). In other words, philosophical hermeneutics is as committed to the process of open conflict as rhetoric is.

We should be wary of any point of view that impedes the criticism of itself. Philosophical hermeneutics commits us to hermeneutical reflection, to the uncovering of our prejudices and the investigating of their power to reveal and conceal. Among these prejudices are the prejudices of philosophical hermeneutics itself. It is important that we read and think about the work of Gadamer, Ricoeur, and other representatives of philosophical hermeneutics, that we attend to them as much as we have to figures such as Derrida and Foucault. It is more important to inquire into the limitations of their prejudices.

We would do well, for example, to listen to Habermas when he asserts that Gadamer's deep concern for communicative action per se tends to ignore how communication is prestructured by political and economic forces (1986, 272-73). To put it bluntly, Gadamer needs to reckon more than he does with *Realpolitik*. It is not enough to respond, with Gadamer, that philosophical hermeneutics does not exclude political and economic critique (1986, 288). Like comic drama, dialogue strives to include rather than exclude, but no dialogue and no amount of dialoguing can be all-inclusive—a fact both logistical and political. Dialogue is necessary but not sufficient in itself; political action in behalf of those systematically excluded from the dialogue is also required. Political action against the suppressors of dialogue—and they are many and have much power in and out of the academy—will also be required. There is, then, amid the charity of philosophical hermeneutics, amid what might seem the naïveté of a hermeneutics of tradition, a political agenda with emancipatory intent.

Are there blind spots and even disabling biases in Gadamer? Assuredly. For instance, besides not attending enough to the domain of work and political struggle, his depiction of method does not reckon with its contemporary diversity and its increasing lack of self-assurance (Weinsheimer 1985, 2-3). Method has become more modest in its own claims. But amid his blind spots and disabling biases, Gadamer does not deprive himself of the pressure of the other by meeting the other as someone to be unmasked or deconstructed. We need not be wary of philosophical hermeneutics because it impedes the criticism of itself. It is not only tolerant of rhetorics different from its own, but demands of itself a listening for the truth claims of all rhetorics.

II Philosophical Hermeneutics and Composition

5 Hermeneutical Rhetoric: The Basic Propositions

What we have so far amounts to a set of commonplaces, the basic *topoi* of philosophical hermeneutics, plus several arguments about its significance in the context of philosophy in general and hermeneutical and rhetorical thought specifically. The task of part two is to sketch a hermeneutical rhetoric. This chapter advances an argument for assimilating hermeneutics to rhetoric. The next chapter begins the process of assimilation itself, exploring the philosophical and theoretical ties between philosophical hermeneutics and one kind of new rhetoric. Finally, the last chapter shows what thinking and teaching composition hermeneutically might mean in more concrete, practical terms.

We focus now on a brief for hermeneutical rhetoric, three propositions with commentary.

All rhetorical acts are also and irreducibly hermeneutical acts.

What this means is that to compose is to interpret, no matter the kind of discourse. The role of hermeneutics is perhaps most salient in arguments about textual meanings, but interpretation is equally significant in even the most straightforward and disinterested presentation of "the facts" about any subject matter. For "raw data" are collected according to some rationale, some set of leading questions, and then further interpreted by what writers select from the total body of available information and what they emphasize in presentation. At no point do we encounter an unmediated reality, but always (at minimum) our own, mostly tacit and inarticulate, preunderstanding of reality. Hence rhetorical acts are *irreducibly* hermeneutical, even in discourses where interpretation itself is not at issue.

This first proposition is only a more restricted version of the claim to universality advanced by philosophical hermeneutics. Ontological hermeneutics advances the unrestricted claim that where there is human-being-in-the-world (*Dasein*) there is at least an implicit, preconceptual grasp of both human being and the world (human existence is always an interpreted existence). Hermeneutical rhetoric need only claim that discourse and composing processes are interpretative through and through.

If rhetorical acts are also hermeneutical acts, then any explicit rhetorical theory or approach to teaching writing is incomplete without a theory of interpretation.

To avoid oversimplification, we must think of the relation between rhetoric and hermeneutics in a twofold, deliberately inconsistent way. They are both separate and intertwined, distinguishable and indistinguishable.

On the one hand, if we take rhetoric as the act or art of discursive composition, then hermeneutics as text interpretation is its companion act or art. If we forget their distinctness, we lose their distinctive functions. Hermeneutics cannot substitute for rhetoric; it is not an art of composing, of invention, arrangement, style, editing, and so on. Rhetoric cannot substitute for hermeneutics; it is not the theory or practice of interpretation. As writers we are rhetoricians and can profit from conscious knowledge of rhetorical art; as readers we are interpreters and can profit from conscious knowledge of hermeneutical art.

On the other hand, whether as spontaneous performance, calculated art, or something of both, rhetoric and hermeneutics merge. Rhetorical invention or discovery never begins from scratch or transpires in a vacuum. On the contrary, our interpretation of the task at hand—subject matter, purpose, genre, readership, and context of situation in particular—predisposes us to inquire within a relatively limited range of questions, problems, and data. More fundamentally, our preunderstandings—our mostly inarticulate experience with writing, including all the discourse variables just mentioned—prestructures more conscious interpretations of the task at hand and largely determines what we find to say. Rhetorical invention, like all forms of inquiry, is always already situated in the writer's life-world, which means that even something so unstructured as free writing is not really unconstrained, not really "free" at all.

Because all phases of composing always go on within interpretative horizons, I have argued elsewhere that the art of rhetoric amounts to "tactical hermeneutics" (Crusius 1989, 153), selection of means based on preunderstanding and conscious interpretation. Of course, no less than invention, disposition and style likewise cannot be detached from interpretative horizons. Insofar as genuine choice exists, it exists as interpretations of appropriateness or effectiveness—that is, the best division of this subject matter, the best presentational order for this readership, the best word, figure, or sentence type for this place in the discourse, and so on.

When we intervene in a student's composing process, what we are seeking to alter is an interpretative horizon within which a certain possibility of choice already exists. The student necessarily brings his or her constructions to the writing class as views of self, the nature of reality, the value of writing, the expectations of English teachers, and so forth. Insofar as these constructions unduly limit or disable what a student can do with the written word, our task becomes both a deconstructing and a reconstructing. Virtually everything we do in a writing class partakes of this dialectical rhythm of tearing down and building up, from seemingly trivial matters like "You may use 'I' in writing personal narrative" to our overall strategies for convincing students that they have something to say and that we are responding to what they are saying, not merely to the correctness of their linguistic forms. In short, hermeneutical rhetoricians mount direct and indirect inquiries into the disabling prejudices of their students with the aim of reconstructing interpretative horizons to permit a wider, more appropriate, and more effective range of rhetorical choice.

If rhetoric cannot account for itself without confronting the general problem of interpretation, then one of our prime concerns should be understanding interpretation itself—exactly the aim of philosophical hermeneutics.

This proposition advances a restricted claim for privileging philosophical hermeneutics over the other four types discussed in chapter one—naïve, normative, scientific, and negative hermeneutics. I am saying, in effect, that rhetorical theory should base its understanding of understanding on Heidegger, Gadamer, Ricoeur, and their followers, rather than on traditional textual hermeneutics, deconstruction, neo-Marxist or neo-Freudian interpretation, and the like. For various reasons in various contexts we can and should use an array of interpretative frameworks, but our general theoretical problem, understanding the role of all interpretative horizons in any discursive act or art, is best advanced not by a specific way of "reading," but by a philosophy of "reading" itself. Philosophical hermeneutics operates at a level of abstraction congenial to modern rhetorical theory's concern with the whole domain of discourse and the entire process of writing.

My third proposition is only another way of expressing a claim first advanced in chapter one—that is, that philosophical hermeneutics subsumes, replaces, or has priority over the other types. The context of assertion, however, is different: earlier the issue was the place of philosophical hermeneutics within hermeneutics generally; here the issue is the appropriateness of privileging philosophical hermeneutics within rhetorical theory.

Let me add two points of clarification. First, my argument for privileging philosophical hermeneutics is not an argument for preferring, say, Heidegger's interpretation of Nietzsche or Gadamer's of Plato over, say, Derrida's readings of the same figures. Working from the perspective of philosophical hermeneutics does not, of course, necessarily lead to superior readings of particular authors or their works (whatever we take "superior" to mean). I did argue near the end of part one that philosophical hermeneutics encourages an attitude of charity and receptiveness toward the truth claims of others, an attitude not consistent with the "we know better" stance of depth or negative hermeneutics. Genuine dialogue with a text or voice is more likely from the stance typical of philosophical hermeneutics, but such a probability hardly guarantees a brilliant or even interesting interpretation of anything.

Second, to grant priority to philosophical hermeneutics in addressing the problem of interpretation intrinsic to rhetorical theory is not to exclude other approaches to interpretative practice or other understandings of interpretation itself. As conceded in part one, Habermas is right to criticize Gadamer for paying too little attention to the role of *praxis* in the Marxist sense—that is, to the world of work and political struggle—in shaping horizons. If part of our task in teaching is deconstructive, a gentle but persistent questioning of student prejudgments, then what we have learned from the hermeneutics of suspicion must play a significant role.

This role, however, is clearly not first or last but secondary and preparatory to reconstruction. It is secondary because the negative moment requires a preexisting construct, an interpretative horizon, for doing its work; it is preparatory because the questioning of horizons is normally not an end in itself. We deconstruct that we may reconstruct, reinterpreting ourselves and the world under the pressure of action that fails to achieve expected outcomes or under the pressure of challenges from other people. Our "first," then, is however we understand what is, has been, and can be now; our "last" is the temporary resting place we reach when we have enlarged or adjusted our horizon to assimilate new experience. The necessity of acting based on some interpretation of how things are—the more or less insistent demands of practical affairs, which is to say, rhetorical affairs—means that we cannot dwell in the deconstructive moment, even if suspension of affirmation is our speculative goal. Undecidability, the condition in which Derrida's dialectic leaves us, may be an appropriate, contemporary response to metaphysics, to claims of an assured foundation for Truth, but it cannot be *Dasein's* dialectic, human being acting in the world.

Dasein's dialectic, rather, is tripartite and Hegelian: existential human being can do nothing else but constantly "assert" its horizons of meaning in thought, speech, writing, and other forms of action; such assertions inevitably encounter resistance in one form or another, including all types of depth critique; in dialogue with the other we transform the negativity of experience into a new positive, a new construct, and the process begins anew. Within this process, writing teachers have several roles to play. They can help students articulate and explore their own interpretative horizons, asking questions, for example, about assumptions, implications, coherence, and consistency. They can deliberately select materials, conceive assignments, and organize the class experience to assure significant challenges to common beliefs and attitudes. They can foster a nondogmatic classroom centered in dialogue, where the negativity of experience can become a genuine challenging of received opinion. And they can assist students in the often painful task of discarding, modifying, and enlarging parts of their interpretative frameworks.

If, in short, we hold with Janet Emig that "writing represents a unique mode of learning" (1988, 85), that rhetoric is epistemic, knowledge-making, not just knowledge-transmitting, then we must also recognize that writing is a hermeneutical process and that the dialectic of reconstruction is central to it. For learning cannot be learning when interpretative horizons remain closed and fixed. And if education does not fundamentally alter human-being-in-the-world, then it is merely training, merely method, not really education at all.

———

To be human is to persuade and be persuaded, to interpret and be interpreted—this is largely what it means to be the symbol-using animal. It follows, therefore, that all students of rhetoric have also been, though seldom consciously, also students of some form of hermeneutic. I have just offered an explicit argument for tying rhetoric and hermeneutics together, but I imagine that the force of this argument resides less in the cogency of the case itself and more in exposing for conscious attention what rhetoricians have been doing all along.

Philosophical hermeneutics is largely dedicated to consciousness-raising, to a phenomenology of interpretation itself; hermeneutical rhetoric is likewise an investigation of what is implicit in rhetorical practice. What we need to do most of all is study ourselves as we write and teach writing. Part of this study—and pivotal to the understanding of rhetorical choice—is the hermeneutical dimension. The specific task of hermeneutical rhetoric is to make inquiry into our (pre- and) understandings integral to acting rhetorically and thinking about rhetorical acts.

6 Assimilating Philosophical Hermeneutics: Theory

In Sum, Thus Far

This study's first part sought, above all, to distinguish a particular kind of hermeneutics, called philosophical or ontological, and to expound its basic concepts and claims in a way that might motivate more students of rhetoric and composition to read Heidegger, Gadamer, and Ricoeur with as much care as they have read currently more fashionable philosophers such as Derrida and Foucault. More specifically, I argued the following:

1. As an interpretation of interpretation itself, philosophical hermeneutics can claim logical priority to any specific "school" or way of reading.

2. As a general, contemporary philosophy of human existence, philosophical hermeneutics is postmodern in the sense of overcoming both traditional metaphysics and epistemology, but its way of engaging the tradition is through retrieval rather than deconstruction. In other words, for those looking for a philosophy that is neither a repetition of the past nor a wholesale rejection of the Western inheritance, philosophical hermeneutics offers a coherent and negotiable position.

3. As a philosophy for contemporary rhetoricians, philosophical hermeneutics commits us to the question, to inquiry, to an ongoing dialogue with experience. If our rhetoric is a rhetoric of inquiry, then we require a hermeneutic of inquiry, not one committed in advance to some single school of interpretation.

4. As a philosophy with a definite educational intent and agenda, philosophical hermeneutics shares with the rhetorical tradition a focus on *phronesis*, on practical judgment, which deals with issues where certainty cannot be achieved. Rhetoric and philosophical hermeneutics, that is, both cultivate the experienced or nondogmatic person, open to exchange with others and aware of "effective history," the situatedness of one's own views, not in eternal verities or self-evident truth, but in the contingencies of

time and circumstance, the relativity of dynamic and conflicting traditions.

In sum, I am urging contemporary rhetoric to pursue an alliance with philosophical hermeneutics rather than with traditional hermeneutics, whether normative or scientific, or the currently influential versions of negative hermeneutics.

In chapter five I made explicit an argument implicit in part one, a case for a self-consciously hermeneutical rhetoric. First, I claimed that all discursive acts are also and irreducibly hermeneutical acts, and that, therefore, any adequate rhetorical theory purporting to account for discourse must advance a theory of interpretation. And second, I argued that philosophical hermeneutics is the best theory of interpretation for our purposes, not because of some innate superiority over other, competing theories, but rather because it engages the general problem of interpretation. Traditional hermeneutics is for the most part a text hermeneutic, and negative hermeneutics usually has an even narrower focus, as in Derrida's case, philosophical texts. Philosophical hermeneutics, because it takes human being as the being who interprets itself and the world, is not restricted in theory or practice to text interpretation. Writers must "read" many symbols scattered in the world that are not actually texts—for example, readerships, their own motives, and what is appropriate for the occasion or medium of publication. Rhetorical theory therefore requires what philosophical hermeneutics offers, an engagement with the general problem of interpretation.

Assuming, then, that my various arguments for the value of philosophical hermeneutics are at least worth entertaining and their implications worth pursuing further, our problem becomes how exactly to assimilate it to current rhetorical theory and practice. Bringing it within the orbit of more familiar, recent theory is the concern of this chapter, and practice (in the sense of a writing program based in rhetorical hermeneutics) the concern of the next.

Berlin and Kinneavy

Although recent rhetorical scholarship refers fairly often to the hermeneutical tradition (see, for example, Phelps 1983, 1988), only a handful of composition specialists have tried to connect the theory or teaching of writing with philosophical hermeneutics specifically. Of these few, two stand out: James L. Kinneavy and James Berlin. Kinneavy was the first to discuss the relationship at any length, and his two articles devoted to hermeneutical rhetoric, both of which develop a Heideggerian view of the composing process, are unquestionably the most significant contribution so far. Berlin, the other noteworthy contributor, explicitly associates hermeneutics with his extensive discussions of the rhetoric-as-epistemic movement. This and the next chapter are heavily indebted to these two scholars, without whom my work would have been much more difficult.

In their explorations of hermeneutics and rhetoric, Kinneavy and Berlin engage both theory and practice. Nevertheless, because Kinneavy centers his attention on the composing process, I have found his work more relevant to the teaching of writing, and so have reserved it for the next chapter. Berlin's investigations of the philosophical and political assumptions and implications of current rhetorical theories are more purely theoretical, and consequently will receive attention in this chapter. Of special interest are the characteristics of what Berlin initially calls epistemic and later social-epistemic rhetoric, because my conception of hermeneutical rhetoric resembles it while departing from it in several crucial ways.

Drawing almost exclusively from Berlin's most recent published essay, "Rhetoric and Ideology in the Writing Class" (1988b), I will first summarize his discussion of social-epistemic rhetoric. Then I will investigate the parallels between his category and what I mean by hermeneutical rhetoric. A subsequent section then highlights our differences. By the end of the chapter we ought to have a firm grasp of hermeneutical rhetoric's "family resemblances," its near of kin among rhetorical theories, as well as a more specific understanding of its individuality, its distinctive way of thinking about discourse and language.

Social-Epistemic Rhetoric

In social-epistemic theory, rhetoric is "a political act involving a dialectical interaction engaging the material, the social, and the individual writer, with language as the agency of mediation" (488).

Rhetoric is a political act because it is unavoidably ideological; that is, the speaker or writer necessarily works from his or her preexisting notion of reality, which amounts to answers to three questions: "What exists? What is good? What is possible?" (479). Because there can be no final or objective answers to these questions, all reality constructions are ideological. No philosophical or scientific discipline, including classical Marxism, which attempts to contrast itself with the "false consciousness" of ideology, "can lay claim to absolute, timeless truth" (478).

The rhetorical act is a dialectical interaction because it cannot be explained by any simple or single cause. Writers are the agents of their acts, but they speak or write out of economic, social, and political contexts that crucially influence the act itself and yet do not strictly determine its features. The writer cannot be detached from her or his role, which, of course, is social, and the available roles do not exist independently of material conditions, especially the realm of work or production. Consequently, no linear cause-effect model can account for discourse; we must resort instead to an interactive model of variables entangled beyond extrication in each other.

The material, social, and individual are all mediated by language because, apart from language, we have no access to them. As Britton explains, "This [mediation by language] does not mean that the three do not exist apart from language: they do. This does mean that we cannot talk and write about them—indeed, we cannot know them— apart from language" (488).

The "social" in social-epistemic theory, then, designates the conflic- tual arena both of rhetorical action and of truth. Social-epistemic rhetoric, in other words, denies that we first discover the truth intuitively or by method and then employ rhetoric as a means of expression or presentation. Rather, "since language is a social phe- nomenon that is a product of a particular historical moment, our notions of the observing self, the communities in which the self functions, and the very structures of the material world are social constructions" (488)—which is to say, always already rhetorical, notions that we hold because we belong to various language commu- nities. Such a view contrasts sharply with what Berlin calls cognitive- epistemic rhetoric (480–84), which attempts to transcend the historical moment by the structuralist appeal to the relative constant of the brain, the biological foundation of thought processes allegedly shared by all human beings.

The "epistemic" in social-epistemic has nothing to do with episte- mology as the Descartes-Kant-Locke tradition understands episte- mology. Since all truths are rhetorical and ideological, the search for a truth foundation, for some ground of incontestable truth, is a misguided quest. The task instead is critique of ideology itself. Berlin suggests questions like the following: "What are the effects of our knowledge? Who benefits from a given version of the truth? How are the material benefits of society distributed? What is the relation of this distribution to social relations? Do these relations encourage conflict?

To whom does our knowledge designate power?" Clearly, then, as Berlin goes on to say, "social-epistemic rhetoric," far from seeking some basis of indubitable truth, "views knowledge as an arena of ideological conflict" (489) and therefore "offers an explicit critique of economic, political, and social arrangements" (490).

This critique is meant to empower students by, first, making them aware of why things are as they are and then, second, by way of this understanding, to see that current arrangements have not always existed and can be altered. If, that is, we can understand the often concealed forces at work in maintaining the current economic and social dispensation, then we can also perceive how the system might be changed: the movement is from consciousness-raising to at least potential social action. In "placing the question of ideology at the center of the teaching of writing," social-epistemic rhetoric takes "the liberated consciousness of students" as "the only educational objective worth considering" (492).

So far as this study is concerned, the value of Berlin's theory resides in a clear and powerful statement of a rhetoric based on depth or negative hermeneutics, which, as we have noted before, is philosophical hermeneutics' main competitor in our present intellectual scene. The contemporary Marxism that undergirds Habermas's contribution to the much-discussed debate with Gadamer also informs Berlin's contribution to the theory and practice of social-epistemic rhetoric, just as Gadamer's philosophy supports my whole argument for hermeneutical rhetoric. In juxtaposing social-epistemic with hermeneutical rhetoric, then, we are about to see how the larger intellectual struggle between conflicting hermeneutical philosophies plays out within the smaller arena of modern rhetorical theory.

Convergences

It is crucial that we first appreciate the large measure of overlap or agreement that pulls the two theories together in common assent to a set of propositions about rhetoric. The following are the most important propositions uniting the two theories.

"Rhetoric is always already ideological" (477).

We can trace to the ancient Greeks the strongly entrenched notion that rhetoric is a free form of power, neutral or uncommitted in that the art is potentially open to and used by everyone regardless of the ideology entertained. Put another way, we tend to think of rhetorical art the way Aristotle apparently did, as a practice that can be dispassionately described quite apart from the ideology of the describer.

Berlin inverts the traditional relationship, "situating rhetoric within ideology, rather than ideology within rhetoric" (477). Hermeneutical rhetoric must assent to this reversal because any understanding of rhetoric—any explicit theory or art of rhetoric—can only be based on preunderstanding, part of which is certainly what Berlin, drawing on Goran Therborn's conception, means by ideology (478–79). In Heideggerian terms, ideology, rationalized or unrationalized answers to the questions What exists? What is good? What is possible? belongs to the ground plan of a language community and to the foresight and foreconception of its members. Preunderstanding is more than ideology—crucially more, as we shall see—but there can be no question that hermeneutical rhetoric must agree that rhetoric and theories of rhetoric are always already ideological. Since, as Aristotle's survey of the *topoi* shows, we persuade in part by appealing to what our audience considers actual, desirable, and practicable, it makes better sense to situate rhetoric within ideology than to imagine rhetoric as a self-contained, free-floating art appropriated by various ideologies.

Furthermore, it is simply not the case that rhetorical art and forums are open to all equally. Human beings are in their very being interpreters and persuaders, but it does not follow from this ontology that everyone has the same opportunity to influence events. Here, Foucault's studies of regimes of power generally—sustained, of course, by ideology—are indispensable to understanding rhetorical power specifically.

The implications of situating rhetoric within ideology are many and significant, especially for our approach to rhetorical texts and the history of rhetoric. And yet, when we assent to Berlin's proposition, we remain solidly within the rhetorical tradition. Since Gorgias and Plato at least, rhetorical theory has been seeing discourse acts within situational contexts. What, then, should prevent us from seeing our own tracts about rhetoric as likewise situated? To say that rhetoric is always already ideological is to say that it is profoundly social, that it is the discourse of our most collective concerns. And what rhetorician from the Sophists on would dispute that?

Whether consonant with the rhetorical tradition or not, however, there can be no question that hermeneutical rhetoric must assent enthusiastically to Berlin's strong claim that "a rhetoric cannot escape the ideological question, and to ignore this is to fail our responsibilities as teachers and as citizens" (493). If, as Gadamer claims, "the real power of hermeneutical consciousness is to see what is questionable" (1976b, 13), then surely notions of the real, the good, and the possible fall within what must be seen as always questionable. Hermeneutical rhetoric may take up the question of ideology in a different way from social-epistemic rhetoric, but it cannot be true to itself and avoid the question.

"Rhetoric is an historically specific social formation that must perforce change over time; and this feature in turn makes possible reflexiveness and revision" (488).

If we situate rhetoric within ideology, then we will expect it to alter as ideologies change. Moreover, as the ideological sources of persuasive appeal shift in nature or emphasis, past sources become more salient by contrast, more subject to conscious scrutiny—hence the connection between temporal transformation and reflexiveness and revision.

Social-epistemic rhetoric, Berlin says, "includes an historicist orientation" (488) crucial to its purposes. That is, in referring all rhetorics to "historically specific social formations," we thereby avoid any temptation to reify some one rhetoric into "the Truth" against which all previous or subsequent rhetorics are evaluated. There can be no transcendent standards in social-epistemic rhetoric.

A central premise of hermeneutical rhetoric is that Being has a temporal structure; therefore, like social-epistemic rhetoric, it cannot invoke any transcendent standard. Hermeneutical rhetoric has no quarrel with Berlin's move from ideology to historical relativity and thence to the openness to critique that an abandoning of traditional metaphysics and epistemology encourages.

However, hermeneutical rhetoric is not precisely historicist; its concern, rather, is with the *historicity* of human existence, an emphasis quite different in its implications. For now, however, the point is that social-epistemic and hermeneutical rhetoric come together in the poststructuralist reaffirmation of historical studies, with all that implies about claims for transtemporal verities. And partly because of a shared emphasis on history, both theories stress reflexiveness and reflection. For both, the unexamined life is not only not worth living, but also philosophically and politically suspect.

"In studying rhetoric—the ways discourse is generated—we are studying the ways in which knowledge comes into existence" (489).

This proposition amounts to an unqualified rejection of any hiatus between language and knowledge, language and rhetoric. Knowledge is always discursive; discourse is always rhetorical: the view of rhetoric common since Descartes—that it is a mere packaging of the truth, a mere presentational art that depends on philosophy or science for epistemic dimension—is here discarded and replaced with the widespread contemporary understanding of philosophy and science as being themselves rhetorical. "Rhetoric is epistemic," Berlin says elsewhere, "because knowledge itself is a rhetorical construct" (1987, 165). Assertions like this are among the key assumptions of recent scholars engrossed with various philosophical and scientific rhetorics.

Although hermeneutical rhetoric must insist that the question of being or existence is prior to questions of knowledge, it holds, with social-epistemic rhetoric and much influential recent philosophy (for example, late Wittgenstein), that, in Berlin's words, "language is a social phenomenon" and knowledge a "social construction . . . inscribed in the very language we are given to inhabit" (488). For both understandings of rhetoric, there can be no extralinguistic or extrasocial ground of appeal; for both, then, "knowledge is a matter of mutual agreement appearing as a product of rhetorical activity" (1987, 166). We find what is true for us through dialogical conflict—through arguing with ourselves and others; through this process we make our claims to truth, to knowledge, which are anything but "eternal and invariable phenomena located in some uncomplicated repository" (489).

In sum, social-epistemic and hermeneutical rhetoric come together in

1. Stressing the irreducible linguisticality of human experience
2. Taking language itself as a social and historical phenomenon, used by people acting, not as an abstract, self-contained system of signs
3. Seeing knowledge as a product of rhetorical and dialectical activity

Divergences

It is indisputably clear that what Berlin calls social-epistemic rhetoric and what I call hermeneutical rhetoric are theories of the same general type. Nor is the large measure of shared ground surprising: Berlin's neo-Marxism is a hermeneutic and Berlin himself invokes philosophical hermeneutics in defending his position, saying at one point, for example, that "we are lodged within a hermeneutic circle" (489).

And yet our theories are hardly the same theory. Exactly how they differ and how the choice of one over the other matters must now become the focus of attention. As in the previous section, I offer a set of propositions with commentary.

In hermeneutical rhetoric, the categories of Marxist critique are as open to question as the capitalist ideologies it would critique.

One of the problems for any advocate of depth hermeneutics is justifying his or her own particular framework. As noted earlier, contemporary neo-Marxism has abandoned classical Marxism's claim to scientific truth, and Berlin agrees by supporting Therborn's stance that "the choice . . . is never between scientific truth and ideology, but between competing ideologies" (478), Marxism being necessarily only one of many such "historically specific" constructions. In other words, Berlin recognizes what Habermas addresses as the "legitimation crisis" in contemporary thought—the situation in which no one's categories have any special authority as a privileged access to the truth. For Habermas, the appropriate response to this situation is neither to settle for historical relativism nor to renew philosophical foundationalism's search for a secure basis for belief. Rather, he mounts detailed arguments in support of his critical categories, hoping to gain authority through advancing the best reasons, the most compelling case.

Berlin seems to opt for historical relativism. At least, he offers no specific argument that would justify taking a neo-Marxist stance.

If Berlin does opt for historical relativism, in one way he is being perfectly consistent with his own tenets. For having said that all belief systems are ideologies that arise within a particular socioeconomic order, he cannot privilege Marxism without violating his own explicitly historicist assumptions. He might remain consistent and argue that Marxism has a special hermeneutical relevance to understanding Western capitalism, and certainly his whole essay strongly implies this situational justification, but that is not actually how he defends his Marxist-inspired theory. Instead, he argues that what distinguishes social-epistemic rhetoric from the other theories he discusses is that it "attempts to place the question of ideology at the center of the teaching of writing" (492).

That Berlin's theory foregrounds ideology and that inquiry into the ideologies explicit or implicit in rhetorical theories is worth doing and is facilitated by this foregrounding seems to me beyond question. But his claim that "social-epistemic rhetoric contains within it the means for self-criticism and self-revision" (490) is highly questionable.

At no juncture in "Rhetoric and Ideology"—or, for that matter, any place else in his published work—does Berlin indicate a willingness to question his own Marxist ideology. In failing to do so, his theory suffers both from inconsistency and hermeneutical inadequacy.

Berlin's theory is consistent, we have said, in refusing to equate his own version of neo-Marxism with Truth. That is, he does not exempt his own framework from the premise that all interpretative horizons are historically specific formations. Specifically, he does not endorse Althusser's distinction between Marxist science and capitalist "false consciousness." And yet, having rejected the science-ideology contrast near the beginning of his essay (478), near the end (490) he endorses Ira Shor's strategies for revealing "forms of false consciousness" in the ideologies of students. On Berlin's own terms, to label the contents of anyone's consciousness as false is simply to beg the question, there being no reliable way to discriminate self-deception from genuine insight. In this way, inconsistency creeps into Berlin's discussion.

The underlying problem—the source of Berlin's inconsistency—resides in the conflict between historical relativity and his own strong allegiance to a Marxist hermeneutic. In effect, he privileges Marxist interpretation while offering no grounds for doing so—indeed, while denying that there can be any grounds for doing so. The discarding and then the invoking of "false consciousness" is only one symptom of Berlin's desire to employ a depth hermeneutic without systematic justification of a claim to special insight.

More serious than inconsistency, however, is the lack of self-questioning that results from exempting his own framework from critique. The hermeneutical art, Gadamer says, consists in finding what is questionable, and Berlin displays the art admirably in questions directed at a reigning orthodoxy: for example, "Who benefits from a given version of truth? To whom does our knowledge designate power?" But he does not apply these questions reflexively, so we can only guess who would profit from his version of the truth, who would have power in his best of all possible worlds. Nor does he seem to perceive how questionable his own educational goal is. What thoughtful teacher does not pursue "the liberated consciousness of students" as a prime educational objective? But we need to ask questions that Berlin does not ask. What, for example, does "liberated" mean? Have we liberated students when we lead them to see that the present socioeconomic order is not unalterable, not simply part of the nature of things? Or have we only increased their awareness, while otherwise leaving them more or less where they were, without any clear notion of exactly what needs to be changed and by what means? Worse still, in purporting to liberate students without opening up our own framework for critique, have we only substituted one authority for another?

Of course, no theorist can reasonably be expected to find all the key questions in any given case, especially what is questionable in her or his own theory. Everyone's hermeneutic is always more or less inadequate; no one is in full possession of the art. But social-epistemic rhetoric as Berlin advances it suffers from more than the ineluctable limitations of a finite consciousness; its inadequacy is built into the system as an overcommitment to a single depth hermeneutic. To adapt Orwell's *Animal Farm,* all claims to truth are equal in the sense that all arise as ideologies, but apparently in Berlin's social-epistemic rhetoric some ideologies are more equal than others.

Because hermeneutical rhetoric privileges interpretation itself rather than some mode of interpretation, it must find what is questionable in all horizons. That is, Heidegger's "passion for the question" cannot be restricted to Western metaphysics or the ideologies of late Western capitalism, but must be equally quizzical of new orthodoxies such as feminism, new historicism, deconstruction, and the like, especially when such oppositional viewpoints become orthodoxies themselves. The goal of hermeneutical rhetoric is never-ending inquiry, not the safety and too-easy satisfactions of "political correctness," whether of the right, the left, or the center. In this it differs sharply not only from Berlin's version of social-epistemic rhetoric, but from all rhetorics committed in advance to a single kind of depth critique.

No less than social-epistemic rhetoric, hermeneutical rhetoric insists on posing the question of ideology as one of the central concerns of writing instruction. But to remain true to itself, hermeneutical rhetoric must hold all ideologies open to question, including its own. And so we need to ask now exactly what ideology is implicit in hermeneutical rhetoric. Especially we need to ask: What is its politics?

Hermeneutical rhetoric must espouse an evolutionary approach to social and political change, a William James-style meliorism, not a marginalized stance of cultural protest or resistance.

Another of the many points of contact between Berlin's theory and mine is that we must both own up to certain obvious political embarrassments. For the contemporary Marxist, there is not only the old burden of Stalinism but the new burden of the collapse of institutionalized Marxism. The common perception is that the Marxist experiment is over and a failure, a perception that leaves theorists like Berlin on strategically low ground, unable quite to overcome, no matter how enlightened and modest the new Marxism happens to be, the stigma of association with an agenda for political action that may be noble but "just doesn't work."

For hermeneutical rhetoric, the situation is no better, probably worse. The old burden here is Heidegger's brief but nevertheless damning collaboration with National Socialism. The new burden is the association of philosophical hermeneutics with a reactionary traditionalism, an impression reinforced by Gadamer's attempts to refurbish concepts like prejudice and authority, by Paul Ricoeur's theological writings, and by, more generally, the essentially correct identification of the hermeneutical tradition with a German academic elite. None of this plays well among English professionals for whom tradition increasingly means continuing domination by a culture of white middle- and upper-class males. It all looks terribly suspect.

When politics is at issue—and when is it not?—there is always enough embarrassment to go around, always plenty of opportunity for reductionistic caricature and satire. One such reduction that has no doubt occurred to many readers already is that the difference between social-epistemic and hermeneutical rhetoric is merely the old difference between the Hegelian left and the Hegelian right, the former stressing the dialectic's progressive-destructive aspect, the latter its preserving-encompassing one. Such a diagnosis has not only a certain plausibility, but also a long and significant history behind it. I will argue, however, that the difference between us is not quite so easily formulated.

Berlin shares with most contemporary Marxists a lack of confidence in revolution. That is why he confines his agenda to consciousness-raising in the service of a democratic socialism. His faith is not in violent upheaval, but rather in the revolution of consciousness that his "liberatory classroom" would promote. "The students are to undergo a conversion," and here Berlin borrows Ira Shor's words, "from manipulated objects into active, critical subjects," the purpose being "to empower them to become agents of social change rather than victims" (491).

No matter how sympathetic one may be to Berlin's program—what teacher does not want to transform too often passive students into "active, critical subjects"?—one must nevertheless call the whole idea of conversion into question. In the first place, while our egos may want it otherwise, the teacher's task is not to make converts, but to enable students to question not only the mystifications of a social order, but also the motives and perspectives of the demystifiers of that order; otherwise, we at best turn out students who are "active, critical subjects" in only one direction. As I indicated in the last section, the lack of reflexiveness, the failure to mount a critique of the adequacy of its critical framework, is the main objection that hermeneutical rhetoric must lodge against social-epistemic rhetoric.

In the second place, if a rhetoric based in a depth hermeneutic uses the metaphor of conversion, hermeneutical rhetoric must question the appropriateness of the metaphor itself. In seeing why hermeneutical rhetoric resists the rhetoric of conversion, we will also uncover one of the more significant differences between Berlin's theory and mine.

From the standpoint of philosophical hermeneutics, in "attempting to place the question of ideology at the center of the teaching of writing," social-epistemic rhetoric performs a reification of its own. That is, it takes the realm of belief as its focus while omitting the role of the nonconceptual in preunderstanding. As a result, it misconceives the nature of change and underestimates the difficulty of effecting change.

As noted before, ideology—what we think exists, what we think is desirable, and what we think is possible—belongs to the conceptual side of preunderstanding, or at least it does in principle, because ideology, whether explicit or not, is expressible, capable of formulation as a set of propositions. Because ideology can be formulated, it can also be critiqued—hence the relative optimism on Berlin's part that a revolution in consciousness can be efficacious in bringing about significant social change.

But our being-in-the-world—*Dasein*—is much more than ideology. The whole dimension of preunderstanding that Heidegger calls "forehaving"—our thrownness into a welter of preexisting social practices and habits, which are deeply internalized long before any capacity for criticism develops—is missed by the ideological reification. To paraphrase Gadamer, what counts in our forehaving is not so much our thinking and our acting in the sense of conscious design, but what goes on despite our thinking and acting. What goes on is not only in large measure tacit—a "knowing" without knowing—but also nonconceptual and profoundly resistant to adequate formulation, without which critique is impossible. The power of reflection is always, therefore, severely limited; it does, to recall Gadamer's words, "bring before me something that otherwise happens behind my back. Something—

but not everything . . . [for consciousness, *Bewusstsein*] is inescapably more being [*Sein*] than consciousness [*Bewusst*]" (1976b, 38).

Precisely because consciousness is more being than consciousness, so-called conversions must be read skeptically as always very partial, never as completely transforming as we sometimes feel them to be. Change is best understood as an enlarging or modification of horizons, not as the complete "turn about" implied by "con-version." There is no escape from forehaving, no way to surmount our historicity (which cannot be usefully historicized, because it is not a set of conditions that only help to explain circumstances "back then," but rather the accretions overlaying accretions that make us what we are now).

Prophets of all stripes impatient with the slow pace of change in human societies will understandably read hermeneutical rhetoric as merely an elaborate defense of conservatism. If we are caught up beyond willing and doing in our being-in-the-world, as Gadamer holds, then it would seem that any program for change is doomed in advance, unable to cope with the inertia of the past. But hermeneutics does not maintain that change is impossible or undesirable, only that meaningful, sustainable change is gradual, evolutionary, and cannot be effected by critique alone. In short, we can hope to make things better; we cannot hope for wholesale transformation on either the individual or collective level.

Berlin's substitution of a revolution of consciousness for the old Marxist faith in revolution by force of arms leaves us still with the liabilities of conversion-revolutionary thinking, which can only end in frustration and in a cultural marginalism whose resistance to the status quo is unlikely to bear fruit. In contrast, hermeneutical rhetoric entails William James's meliorism, a mainstream American position much more broadly negotiable. The difference, then, between Berlin's theory and mine is not the contrast between Hegel's left and Hegel's right, but faith in the transforming power of critique versus faith in the enlarging and modifying power of hermeneutical inquiry through the conflict of ideologies. Instead of attempting to uproot the unreflective capitalist (racist, sexist, etc.) ideology so many of our students stubbornly adhere to, hermeneutical rhetoric seeks to prune and graft, altering how the tree grows rather than cutting down and burning it and planting anew.

If there is a quarrel between social-epistemic and hermeneutical rhetoric, it is a friendly quarrel, differences within a broadly similar viewpoint. Berlin and I come together most notably in rejecting the scientism of cognitive rhetoric (for example, Flower and Hayes) and in rejecting the radical individualism of expressionistic rhetoric (for example, Murray and Elbow). For both of us, rhetoric is an art, the most social and ideological of the arts; for both of us the key terms are *language* and *time,* which is to say, *being* and *time,* because human being is being in language events, and all being that can be understood is understood in language events.

For hermeneutical rhetoric, however, the various neo-Marxist voices can only be so many peers in a dialogue of many voices— significant but not preemptive, full of insight but hardly its exclusive source. Hermeneutical rhetoric asks us to be open to the Marxist critique even as it asks the Marxist to be open to a critique of the critique offered. In this way, genuine dialogue can go on, putting in question everyone's interpretations, rather than privileging one vocabulary of interpretation over another.

7 Assimilating Philosophical Hermeneutics: Pedagogy

Of all subjects a rhetorician might take up, the hardest to write about is the art of teaching because so much of it is forehaving and personal style, immersion in practices half-understood, less than half-communicable, and undetachable from know-how in the sense of "the right stuff," the whatever-it-is that distinguishes truly gifted teachers from good or competent ones. Moreover, the right stuff is not the same from great teacher to great teacher, so the art of teaching is frustratingly elusive—we know it when we experience it, but as soon as we talk about it, we also know it is constantly slipping away.

This chapter is not about the art of teaching writing, the sort of reaching brilliantly toward the inexpressible that we encounter in Peter Elbow or Donald Murray. Rather, it is about the emphases of hermeneutical rhetoric as I have attempted to put it into practice, both over many years in the classroom and lately as director of the writing program at Southern Methodist University. The latter role has pushed me hard toward articulating the practice of hermeneutical rhetoric, the results of which I offer here.

For me, hermeneutical rhetoric has never been just a theory, but the way I have been teaching composition for about twenty years, since a reading of Kenneth Burke's *Permanence and Change* (1965) first made me aware that interpretation and rhetoric are inseparable. Since then, I have tried to teach rhetoric hermeneutically—or at least I see in retrospect I was trying to do that. ("Hermeneutics" entered my vocabulary only about ten years ago; concentrated reading of hermeneutical philosophy only in the last five; trying to make a conscious rhetorical theory out of it only in the past few years.) I spare the reader all the trials and errors and go straight to where I am now in my continuing effort to translate a theory into the principles guiding a composition program.

A Definition

Hermeneutical rhetoric

    a. aims to deepen the process approach to writing instruction

74

b. by retrieving dialectic as dialogue, as hermeneutical inquiry,

c. within a rhetoric of public discourse emphasis

d. that concentrates on argumentation or the search for "good reasons."

Before I comment on each part of this definition in detail, a few observations about it in general might be helpful.

Parts a and b are indispensable to hermeneutical rhetoric and follow directly from its theoretical commitments. Process is the very heart and soul of philosophical hermeneutics and has been since Heidegger's yoking of being with time. One might even say that philosophical hermeneutics is radically processual; unlike normative or scientific hermeneutics, it looks for the unsettling question, not the settled interpretation.

Retrieving dialectic as hermeneutical inquiry is more Gadamer's project than Heidegger's. The latter explicitly links *Dasein* with *Mitsein* and invokes Holderlin's "dialogue which we are"; but it was Gadamer who unfolded the dialogical implications of ontological hermeneutics to the point where even textual interpretation becomes dialogue rather than the analysis of an artifact.

Parts c and d of my definition are less tightly bound to hermeneutical rhetoric. Since the ancient Greeks, whenever public debate has been permitted in Western societies, one of the principal genres of rhetoric has been deliberation or policy argumentation. A major genre in the United States from the outset, it became, according to Berlin, a conscious emphasis in the writing programs of many of our universities during the Depression years (1987, 81–88) and has since tended to resurface in other times of acute national crisis—as in the Vietnam era. Public discourse engages current and recurrent issues of general concern: among the former, for example (circa late 1990), Should President Bush use the troops in Saudi Arabia to recover Kuwait by force? among the latter, for example, Should abortion remain legal?

Clearly one might emphasize public discourse in a composition program without any commitment to hermeneutical rhetoric or emphasize other kinds of discourse within a commitment to hermeneutical rhetoric. The one hardly entails the other. And yet they are connected.

To see the connection, we need only recall Habermas's linkage of hermeneutics and rhetoric, cited previously in chapter one: "The art of interpretation is the counterpart of the art of convincing and persuading in situations where practical questions are brought to decision" (1989, 294). Practical questions, of course, take in more than issues of popular debate, arising, for instance, in family, institutional, and professional settings of more restricted focus. Nevertheless, because the rhetoric of public discourse engages a society's most collective concerns, it remains paradigmatic of practical questions (that is, policy issues) that cannot be resolved simply by appeal to the knowledge accumulated by specialized fields of study.

It is significant, by the way, that Habermas should take hermeneutics as rhetoric's counterpart, rather than dialectic, Aristotle's candidate for the counterpart relationship. For reasons we will discuss later, the form of dialectic called classical can no longer be adequate as rhetoric's counterpart. Rather, as Gadamer argues, the dialectical function must now fall to hermeneutics, whose philosophical horizon is better suited to postmodern conditions. The retrieval of dialectic as dialogue, as hermeneutical inquiry, then, implies a rereading of classical dialectic.

In part, a rhetoric of public discourse emphasis is implicated in the prominent role that hermeneutics always plays where practical questions are at issue. In part, I have gravitated towards it because public discourse lends itself to hermeneutical inquiry, especially inquiry into ideology, and to other educational objectives, most importantly the cultivation of *phronesis,* or practical judgment, the ability to bring practical questions to decision by recognizing the best case among many competitors. The cultivation of *phronesis,* the educational goal shared by hermeneutics and rhetoric, results in concentration on argument in the sense of "the rhetoric of good reasons" identified with Chaim Perelman (*The New Rhetoric,* 1969), Wayne Booth (*Modern Dogma,* 1974), and others.

My attempt to pull hermeneutics and argumentation together results from several influences and a strong conviction. The most significant influence is Richard Bernstein's reading of Gadamer's *Truth and Method,* in which he holds that the lack of a *sensus communis* in heterogeneous societies like the United States means that one cannot simply appeal to shared norms and values, but rather must argue for the norms and values we invoke as well as for our application of them in addressing practical questions (Bernstein 1986, 99–104). Another influence is Habermas's theory of communicative action, in which validation through argument plays a central role.

The conviction is that universities ought to be places dedicated to rational inquiry, the discourse of which should be dominated by the scrutiny of arguments in the relatively formal, case-making sense— that is, discourse characterized by carefully worded theses, defended by explicit reasons backed by evidence secured by critical research, and a willingness to confront fearlessly its own assumptions and implications. However idealized it may be, this conviction about the function of the academy and the nature of academic discourse has everything to do with the practice of hermeneutical rhetoric, which cannot retrieve dialectic by resort to the rhetoric of public discourse alone. Much public persuasion remains what it was for Aristotle, not very rigorous dialectically, leaning heavily on ethical, pathetic, and stylistic appeal to win assent. We need not denigrate rhetoric's appeal to the whole person, but academe must provide the space and time to think through all convictions, including the commitment to rational inquiry, by no means undisputed in the current intellectual scene.

In sum, hermeneutical rhetoric is not the rhetoric of Madison Avenue, not simply the rhetoric of power, "how to win friends and influence people." It is not, that is, the rhetoric identified, perhaps unfairly, with the Sophists. Nor is it, for all of its attraction to dialogue and dialectic, Plato's rhetoric, aristocratic, authoritarian, rooted in metaphysics. It is closest to Aristotle, who understood rhetoric and dialectic as separate but closely related and interacting arts. But hermeneutical rhetoric has far less faith in system and method than Aristotle did, and no faith in a hierarchy of disciplines that would make science, or metaphysics, or formal logic the best approach to truth. Rather, hermeneutical rhetoric proposes to begin with what we are and where we are, thrown and finite creatures, immersed in a time and place, a certain climate of opinion or prejudice, striving to understand better what we think and why. The goal is the experienced person, open to the lessons of negativity we call experience, nondogmatic in the sense of being ready to place one's own horizon at hazard.

What Is This Thing Called Process?

> Everyone teaches the process of writing, but everyone does not teach the *same* process.
>
> —James Berlin 1988a, 59

No composition professional wants to return to the old theme-a-week composition class, where writing was only assigned and graded, not taught, where interaction with the students was confined for the most part only to formal prescription and the elimination of error. But increasingly in recent years critics of the ubiquitous process approach have questioned the reigning concept of process itself. New rhetoric's left wing has rightly pointed to the neglect of the institutional setting of the writing classroom in process theory, while cautious progressives (that is, meliorists) like me find in it a scientism that detaches process from act and situational context, abstracting to The Composing Process, whereas there are only composing processes, varying greatly from writer to writer and task to task. The most telling critique of process is James Kinneavy's "The Process of Writing: A Philosophical Base in Hermeneutics" (1987), which moves through critique to a revision of the process concept itself.

Granting, as nearly everyone does, that the process method "is immeasurably superior to the cold one-shot products of the traditional paradigm," Kinneavy nevertheless isolates recurrent problems in the method itself. "One of these has been the neglect and disregard, on the part of some, of almost any concern with product at all." He refers to a textbook he reviewed, one of many that could be cited, that "after about four complete chapters," or "about one third of the way through the book," "still had not . . . asked [the students] to compose a whole paper." "Process so enthroned and separated from any relation to product," Kinneavy warns, "can be as meaningless as grammar or vocabulary taught in isolation from the actual act of writing" (1–2).

More important than the excesses of the process method is that "process is often very narrowly conceived." "Many scholars"—Kinneavy cites Emig, Macrorie, Elbow, Flower and Hayes, and Matsuhashi as examples—"have taken it as axiomatic that the act of writing begins when a student puts pencil to paper and starts to produce a sequential manuscript." This view, which fails to attend to what I have called pre-composing (Crusius 1989, 155), the everyday, long-term activities of writers preparing to write, is "totally at variance with the practice of professional writer[s]," who "don't just sit down and begin an exercise in free-writing" (2).

"What [we] need," Kinneavy concludes, "is a much more comprehensive notion of process." He goes on to discuss, in far greater detail than I did in chapter three, Heidegger's theory of forestructure as the best candidate for a more comprehensive notion (3–8). His treatment cannot be summarized here; anyone seriously interested in the concept of process must read and ponder this article carefully. It is the first treatment of process in our field backed by thorough knowledge of a process philosophy.

What is called process? Here is Kinneavy's summation:

> When an author wishes to write about something, to interpret this something to future readers, he or she brings to the act of writing a forestructure. This forestructure is constituted by the entire history of the author, including complex cultural conventions

which have been assimilated. Against this background, the something which is to be written about is interpreted.

... The original forestructure ... is continually modified as the richness of the object [that is, the subject matter] causes the writer to change his or her original views of his or her intention, unity, and structure. (6–7)

In other words, composing processes are hermeneutic circles, within which "both object and forestructure may require radical alterations, even transformations" (7) as we think through what we are writing about before, during, and after actual composition.

If composing processes are hermeneutical circles, what, then, does "teaching process" amount to? What should we be doing in light of *Vorstruktur* or pre-composing?

As hermeneutical rhetoric is not politically radical, so it is also not pedagogically radical. When I said that hermeneutical rhetoric aims to deepen the process approach, I meant enlarge the concept, not overhaul or revolutionize it. A hermeneutical rhetorician teaches process in much the same way that any up-to-date composition teacher does—that is, by multiple drafts, by not only allowing but also encouraging revision, by the use of writing workshops, collaborative learning, and the like. What, then, is distinctive about the practice of hermeneutical rhetoric within what is generally understood by the process method?

If it is true that authors bring their "entire history" to composing, "including complex cultural conventions," as Kinneavy holds, then we must be wary of the process approach or method insofar as it is an approach or a method. On this point Donald Murray speaks for hermeneutical rhetoric well when he claims, "There is no text in my course until my students write. I have to study the new text they write each semester." The task for each student and for each new draft, citing again from Murray, is to find "some new questions." Our students, of course, usually want answers, preferably *the* answer, not questions, to which Murray replies, "I might even have an answer, but if I do I'll be suspicious. I am too fond of answers . . . ; I have to fight the tendency to think I know the subject I teach" (1988, 235, 237).

Why must writing teachers not believe in the process method insofar as it is methodical? Why must we continually remind ourselves that we cannot know our subject? The truth is that we cannot even know our own history, the complex cultural conventions we have internalized; for the most part, we can only live it/them, for we are it/them. Clearly, if our own histories are known only very partially to us, far less can we claim to know the histories of the students we teach.

The point is not so much that arrogance is imprudent, unattractive, and self-deceiving; the point is not even quite the obvious one that each student requires a somewhat different approach. Rather, what is at issue is authenticity as philosophical hermeneutics understands the term, "being ourselves" not in the popular sense of doing what we please, what feels good, but in the unpopular sense of not knowing and knowing that we do not know. Yes, there is a degree of Socratic irony here—at least we had better be more experienced generally and more experienced as writers specifically to merit the role we play, but this irony needs irony to be authentic. We must fight the tendency to think we know the subject we teach, because we cannot know it—not in its entirety, and certainly not in advance of the text the student produces; because process is not process under the illusion of mastery, but merely the latest assembly line (employing, no doubt, the best current technology) for the production of papers; because our task is to find the right questions, and there is no algorithm for the art of questioning, no list of questions that will always be the ones we ought to ask.

The point is, then, that when the process method becomes methodical it becomes inauthentic, perhaps inauthentic in a different way than composition teaching old style, but still ungenuine, not really engaged. The hermeneutical rhetorician wants to be Murray's "listening eye." For if the student's text is not allowed to speak, if we always think that we know better and in advance what the text ought to say, how can we possibly teach our students to listen to their own words, without which Kinneavy's "rich dialectical movement in the hermeneutic back and forth between the object and the interpreter" (7) cannot happen? If we are not listening, how will they learn to listen for the questions implicit in what they have written?

With authenticity on our part comes the possibility of an answering quality of engagement on the part of our students, whom we have invited, in effect, to join in the dance of composing. (Many will have other plans or join in half-heartedly, of course; but suspicion of method and answers at least means that, having given up on mastering the composing process, we have no other choice but to allow it to master us.) And then, if authenticity is possible, another possibility comes into view—that together we might make modest inroads into our collective alienation, the condition that Heidegger called homelessness.

As outrageous and inflated as it may seem at first, teaching process is nevertheless, at bottom, an effort to overcome estrangement. The rising discipline of cultural studies wants to attack alienation head on by making difference itself the subject matter of writing courses, so that we are studying and writing about race, gender, and class issues.

The aim of such a program is a decentering, primarily from Western ethnocentricity, indisputably, if hardly alone among world cultures, racist, sexist, and classist. As we will see further on, hermeneutical rhetoric supports such a program, if somewhat more indirectly and ambivalently than its advocates would like.

From the standpoint of philosophical hermeneutics, however, the cultural studies perspective altogether misses alienation's most pervasive cause, which afflicts everyone regardless of ideology. The problem is that too much of the time we are not participants in a process but rather processed. The problem is the cult of efficiency, the worship of scientific expertise, the intrusion of the technological rationale into every facet of our lives. This mania for engineering everything leaves us without an effective retort: What can one say to assembly lines, to bureaucracies? They just move on, doing what they do inexorably, not listening and not asking. Even on those rare occasions when we do interact with this world that method has created, our saying is already coopted: we don't have conversations; we have input. The result is not a dialogue, but output, something measured in the same way our "progress" in the Vietnam war was assessed, by counting bodies.

The graceless accountant's mentality dominates education as well. It is all for the counting: How much did you publish last year? How many student credit hours did you generate? For the most part—we ought to confess it, for this realization is the beginning of genuine educational reform rather than mere tinkering—we process students rather than teach them. Are they alienated from learning? How could they be otherwise? They are just passing through a system that tells them what courses to take, what books to buy, what lectures to listen to, what to write, even, in some cases, what kind of paper to write on, what margins to set, where to place their names (top right-hand corner, is it? And don't forget your student number!).

Homelessness, alienation should not be for us only an abstract term from existential philosophy. We see it almost every day in the student who turns up at our office, paper in hand, wanting to know and sometimes asking in so many words, "Is this what you want?" Here is despair, pure and simple, naked and pathetic. What we need to do is counter with Murray's questions, the hermeneutic ones that have potential for dialogue: "What did you learn from this piece of writing? What do you intend to do in the next draft?" and so on (1988, 234). The first step is to ask for their interpretations and thereby perhaps to gain an active partner, without which no dialogue is possible. And with activity comes the potential for repossessing the world that being processed has taken away, almost beyond the thought of questioning.

This is what empowering students ought to mean: nurturing authority itself, not substituting one kind of indoctrination for another, one
kind of unquestioned authority for another.

Process philosophy arose in part to overcome the dissociations of
metaphysics and epistemology, especially the subject-object dichotomy. Instead of the passive observer detached from an object-world of
events, an onlooker, process philosophy asserts our being-in-the-
world, our participation in events. Our own dedication to process
needs more study in the context of process philosophy—and not just
Heidegger's. Whatever we decide his limitations are for us, however,
we will find in his analysis of *Dasein* something very close to the heart
of teaching process, namely, authentic human-being-in-the-world's
role as the only being who can care and question.

Process is about authenticity, which hardly comes naturally to a
being that has no choice but to live for the most part without reflection,
in the middle of *Mitsein* in the sense of "they," chatty sociability rather
than dialogue. Add to this our contemporary world of flash and dash,
where caring and questioning are often a disadvantage, and we begin
to see why moments of authenticity are so rare and so fragile. Teaching
process is an effort to open a space where genuine engagement is a
little less rare and a little more sustaining.

Retrieving Dialectic as Hermeneutical Inquiry

If we cannot effect an authentic relationship with our students, a
partial overcoming of the passive alienation our educational system
promotes by managing students rather than interacting with them,
then we cannot engage in dialogue with our students, and teaching
process is a sham. Achieving a certain quality of engagement is the first
step—although it is really not a step at all but an entire way of
confronting the other. As David Linge, commenting on Gadamer's
"hermeneutical conversation," explains, dialogue entails "equality
and active reciprocity," all the more important to cultivate because
teacher and student are not social equals in the institutional setting.
"The dialogical character of interpretation," Linge adds, "is subverted
when the interpreter concentrates on the other person as such rather
than on the subject matter—when he [she] looks *at* the other person,
as it were, rather than *with* him [her] at what the other attempts to
communicate" (author's emphasis, 1976, xx). To the extent that
equality and active reciprocity are possible, they come into play when
we look with our students, helping them to probe what they say,

rather than looking at them or their texts as people-things with problems and deficiencies.

(Yes, we will, as standard-setters and grade-givers, have to look at their texts too, but this is late in, or arguably after, the process and apart from the dialogue.)

Assuming that we can open the space for caring and questioning, what comes next? In my view, we cannot stop where Murray seems to stop; his questions, in effect demanding student author-ity, are necessary but insufficient. We need the questions especially that allow us to get at forestructure, the practices and ideologies of our students as revealed in their texts. That is, we need dialogue, but as dialectic.

When Gadamer said that "dialectic must retrieve itself in herme-neutics" (1976a, 99), he had in mind Hegel's dialectic, not Plato's. As explained in chapter three, by retrieving dialectic Gadamer means holding on to Hegel's phenomenology but discarding his metaphys-ics. Hegel's descriptions of the process of increasing self-under-standing are very close to Gadamer's dialectic of experience, in that "assertions" (horizons of meaning) are constantly challenged by the anomalous and by other, conflicting horizons, resulting optimally in a dialogical process akin to *Aufhebung,* a modifying-enlarging of horizons to encompass "new matter." Basically, Gadamer is attracted to Hegel's destruction-reconstruction rhythm, but not to the method (its claims for a necessary sequence) or to its teleology. (For Gadamer, the process is endlessly recurrent and unpredictable, Absolute Spirit being impos-sible for finite and fallible human being.)

Understood via Gadamer's retrieval of it, Hegel's dialectic is crucial to teaching composition, because part of our work, especially in what I have called the "stage-managing" aspect of process teaching (Crusius 1989, 154–55), is to assure as much opportunity as possible for the challenging of horizons (our own as well as the students'). One reason I emphasize the rhetoric of public discourse is that I have found no other emphasis that solicits assertion and counterassertion better or confronts us so insistently with inconvenient data and viewpoints resistant to easy assimilation.

Dialectic in Hegel's sense certainly illuminates part of what is going on in a vital writing class, but because most of our students lack strategies for questioning discourse, a retrieval of dialectic in Plato's sense is also helpful. Classical dialectic, as exemplified, for example, in Aristotle's *topoi,* requires retrieval for many reasons—because some of the topics are no longer relevant; because in at least one of its moods it nurtures the contentiousness of debate rather than the openness of inquiry; and because the theory of language implicit in it is by contemporary standards outmoded and too metaphysical. Employed, however, within a modern understanding of language and with an attitude appropriate to discovery rather than self-defense, some of its places can help students see both what they have said and what they need to say. If we really want students to think for themselves, as we often claim, classical dialectic provides a powerful instrument, the basic questions of which are relatively easy for us to teach and for our students to apply on their own.

Classical dialectic is fundamentally an effort to specify how opinions may be questioned. Because an opinion takes the form of statements or propositions, we can question the key terms in which it is expressed; or we can try to expose what is not said for scrutiny, through either inquiry into its assumptions, what lies "behind" the opinion, or into its implications, what lies not yet realized "in front of" the opinion.

Recently, in the aftermath of a program designed to inform students about "safe sex," I decided to attempt a push beyond mere instrumentality to the question of right and wrong by asking my class to articulate and defend their sexual ethics. Already, merely in explaining the topic, I was teaching dialectic, for we had to ask, for instance, what qualifies as sexual expression and what ethics amounts to. (As I explained to my class, the question asks them to defend what they think people ought to do, not necessarily what they do. I did not want a "true confessions" paper about their sexual practices; rather, I wanted them to think through their moral convictions. I also wanted them to see that an ethic cannot be merely personal or individual, as many of my students profoundly wanted it to be. Rather, in saying what is right and wrong, we are at least making claims about our own society, the group of people with which we associate.)

I was surprised to discover that fully a third of my students wanted to defend the proposition that sexual intercourse should be confined to a marital relationship. I was not surprised that this group, even after a brainstorming session during which they were supposed to produce reasons in support of the position, had not gone very far in exploring its assumptional background. All I had to ask was: What is it about marriage, as distinct from any long-term, monogamous relationship, that makes sexual intercourse right? They had to reckon with the sacramental assumptions surrounding marriage in traditional faith, the fuller meaning of which is hard for a denizen of our time to understand. Several students discovered at this point that they were not actually saying what they meant to say; for them, the issue was not really marriage per se, but the quality of feeling and commitment between the partners that mattered. It was time for them to reformulate their thesis and search for a new set of reasons. For the others, my question brought to light the unsaid in their saying, a whole line of defense that really had to be said. Their position required it.

I also wanted those still holding to the linkage of sex with marriage to reckon with some of its implications as well as its assumptions. Can a meaningful distinction be drawn between intercourse and other forms of sexual expression? Were they truly willing to marry someone they had not slept with? Should their spouse lose interest in sex or in sex with them or become too ill to have it, did they still believe in remaining faithful? And so on.

The point of all these questions, of course, was not to suggest that "waiting until marriage" was a bad or indefensible position. On the contrary, our discussions produced the rudiments of a strong case, the details of which they had to work out individually. I should add that all positions advanced were subject to scrutiny—no group was "picked on," singled out as in special need of help. (Which is not to say that all positions turned out to be equally strong—the question of the relative value of different arguments we shall consider under the last rubric, "good reasons.")

The point was to reveal some of the forestructure of strongly felt beliefs, to show that opinions can be questioned and questioned effectively, to provide, not a method of generating questions, but an illustration of the "places" where questions may be found. We look into the range of meanings that a key word has in general usage, into distinctions like that between marriage and monogamy, into assumptional backgrounds, into "what follows" if we accept proposition X rather than Y. And the point is not only to illustrate the places, but to talk consciously about them, so that the students can see where our questions come from and begin to use the places themselves. The point is to offer them the tools for thought.

The initial task, then, is to establish the trust and mutuality essential to authentic dialogue—here, Murray's kind of question should predominate. If we can achieve some degree of genuine involvement, then the way is open to classical dialectic's contribution, the art of questioning in the sense of examining opinions. But classical dialectic is limited in what it can do. For example, the position linking marriage and sexual intercourse needs to reflect on marriage purely as a human institution, as a legal contract, a social custom with norms of practice having definite economic and political implications—which is to say, nonsacramentally. Here we need to ask the kinds of questions Berlin poses—for example, "Who benefits from a given version of truth [or of what is good, or right, or desirable]? To whom does our knowledge [or our opinion of what ought to be] designate power?" (1988b, 489).

Since the task of classical dialectic is to probe opinions, quite literally, on their own terms, it cannot do the job of ideology critique, which questions an opinion "from the outside," seeking to bring to light not what is assumed or implied by a thesis, but rather what the thesis does not say in a different sense, the possible perspectives it omits or deemphasizes. We all need this kind of challenge, if only to mature our position, but clearly we are not ready for it until we understand the assumptions and implications of our own opinion. The point for the hermeneutical rhetorician is this: If the challenge from the outside does not arise spontaneously in class discussions, it is the teacher's task to pose the questions that will bring it into play.

Where, we may want to ask, should hermeneutical questioning stop? When are we finished with it? If we have Heidegger's passion for questioning, we will not stop and will never finish until we are really "finished"—dead or its living equivalent. In practical terms, however, we have to stop somewhere, somewhen. It seems to me that, having discriminated at least the major stances taken on an issue, having scrutinized what each stance assumes and implies, and having made sure that no stance has managed to dodge its other, the dialectician has done his or her work. It is time to write and to find new questions over evolving drafts, the sort of questions the "listening eye" finds itself asking. And so we are back to Murray.

The Rhetoric of Public Discourse

I have indicated already that the public discourse emphasis is neither necessary nor arbitrary where the practice of hermeneutical rhetoric is concerned. Other kinds of discourse, even those that are not argumentative or persuasive, are open to hermeneutical practice. And yet, because public discourse is paradigmatic of the practical question, where we must "convince and illuminate without being able to prove"—to once again recall Gadamer's description of the purpose shared by rhetoric and hermeneutics—the choice does not come down only to my preference, but reflects a certain kinship or natural attraction. Hermeneutical rhetoric is most at home in the conflict of interpretations, the ideological struggles, of public discourse.

A full-scale defense of the public discourse emphasis would require another book and is somewhat beside the point of an introduction to philosophical hermeneutics. In lieu of that defense, I will offer a brief list of advantages:

1. Our students often seem indifferent to and even alienated from public policy issues. Such concerns need to become part of their world, part of the caring and questioning of being human, of being an adult, a citizen.

2. Apart from some speech courses, usually not required of all students, the rhetoric of public discourse is not likely to be taught if we do not teach it.

3. Exposure to the give-and-take of public discourse is good training both intellectually and attitudinally for a democratic society, where practical decisions have to be made in the midst of uncertainty and deeply felt conflict. Any contempt our students may have or acquire during their university experience for "mere opinion" or "mere talk" needs to be undermined.

4. Engagement with public discourse is one of the best routes for cultivating practical judgment in its fuller dimensions. Our students must learn how to listen in the sense of how to assess the conflicting opinions they will encounter as they assume positions of leadership and authority.

For these and other reasons, I think our composition programs ought to have a substantial commitment to the rhetoric of public discourse. As we shall see, however, this emphasis is unlikely to bear fruit apart from a concern with "good reasons." And so with this concern we will end our discussion of the practice of hermeneutical rhetoric.

Why "Good Reasons"?

The search for good reasons dominates invention in a rhetoric of public discourse centered in argument or case-making. Once we understand what we want to argue, then our task becomes finding the reasons that both justify our stance and constitute part of our appeal for the adherence of others. As important as this discovery role is, however, "good reasons" plays several other roles of no less importance.

In stressing the projection of horizons, hermeneutical rhetoric can only begin where the students are, with the opinions they already hold. In trying to create a classroom and conference environment where opinions can be challenged, where no opinion escapes critique, hermeneutical rhetoric hopes to see at least the refining of initial opinions into defensible theses. Actually, it hopes for more than that: through questioning, not telling, it wants to lead students toward detecting opinions that should not just be refined, but rather discarded; it wants students who have defensible positions to recognize when someone else's argument is better, when they ought to assent to another position not their own. In other words, hermeneutical rhetoric takes one of the central questions posed by good reasons very seriously: When should I change my mind?

Thirteen years ago (1978), a first-year class of mine at the University of North Carolina at Greensboro chose as their topic, "Should homosexuals be allowed to teach in the public schools?" It is not hard to guess what happened. With a few exceptions, the students wanted to answer, in thunder, "No!" Because I do not permit myself the role of counter-indoctrinator, I had no choice but to lead an exploration of the topic, isolating the issues it raises, and then to send the students off to the library equipped with a set of questions we hoped our research would answer.

After a week's work, they returned in acute distress. Nothing they had found supported "No!" in whispers, much less in thunder. Some were sullenly determined to hold their position anyway; more were clearly pulled between heartfelt belief on the one hand, and the data on the other. One or two of the latter group actually came to my office in tears.

They had found, among other facts distressing to them, that, if one was worried about the sexual abuse or seduction of public school students, the group to be worried about was heterosexual males, not homosexuals. The overwhelming majority of known instances of sexual relations between students and teachers followed the pattern we know so well at colleges and universities: male instructors, female students. Yes, there were some instances of homosexual activity, but not enough to support a case. Moreover, while many students seemed to think that homosexual teachers would proselytize, the evidence suggested, on the contrary, that almost all simply wanted to go about the business of teaching their subject, pursuing their love interests, like most other people, after hours and in private with partners appropriate to their age and station.

Most homosexuals who had teaching jobs seemed, for good reason, to fear exposure most of all; seeking converts by bringing the good news to their students was apparently furthest from their intentions. In any case, it was also clear that, even if a homosexual teacher approached a student with Iago-like powers of insinuation, a student's sexual orientation was not likely to be affected by it. And then, even if a case could be made against the homosexual teacher, there was the apparently insurmountable problem that certain generally recognized rights based on the Constitution made it impossible to determine a teacher's sexual preference. And so on, and so on: by the time our discussion of the research was over, the students with their thunderous "No!" had little left but their homophobia to work with.

Donald Murray claims to be "uncomfortable when his students are uncomfortable, but more uncomfortable when they are comfortable" (1988, 234). I feel the same way, but the mounting agony of my class began to make me feel more like a sadist. So, having allowed a certain amount of the pain necessary when people have to discard cherished opinions, I posed a question I always pose at some point during the semester: When should we change our minds? I explained that the emphasis here is on "should"—not when do we change our minds, but when should we. Clearly, when the preponderance of the evidence suggests that our opinion just does not hold water, we ought to change our minds.

"You mean," asked one of my students, "that we should defend a position we don't believe in?"

"No," I said. "What I mean is that our beliefs ought to change when we find that we cannot make a case for them." I went on to give examples of when I had changed my own opinions and why. "It is admirable to have strong convictions," I concluded, "but not admirable to continue to adhere to them when they prove insupportable."

Philosophical hermeneutics insists on not only the necessity of prejudgment but also on its positive value—without prejudice, we experience nothing. But hermeneutical inquiry is designed to move beyond discovering what our prejudices are to distinguishing between enabling and disabling prejudices. Although in my experience the crisis in my class at Greensboro was unusually intense, a rhetoric of public discourse emphasis combined with research and dialectic always challenges the disabling prejudices of my students, and often mine as well. If this is not what education ought to be—deconstructing and reconstructing under the pressure of what is known and in response to key questions—I have no idea what it should be.

In the instance just described, the disabling prejudice was so disabling that my students could not write until they had overcome it. Disabling prejudices are seldom such a clear barrier and are typically much harder to detect. For most topics, students will eventually discover, if not without many visions and revisions, more or less *prima facie* cases in support of positions that represent refinements of their initial opinions. Because we study these cases in class, the students come to see that good reasons exist for holding opinions that they may have considered insupportable before the process began. This, too, is genuine learning, and as indicated by students I have had as first-year students and again later as juniors or seniors, it is learning that sticks— they do not forget what they have learned when they have had to struggle with a genuine issue. But even this is not enough.

After the papers have been written and rewritten, turned in, marked, graded, and returned, there is one last step in the process, which probably takes good reasons to its outer limit of usefulness. For even the most contested issues, when divisions in the class remain deep, I still like to devote one class at least to trying to answer yet another question: Can we find a position that most of us can support, even if none of us are altogether happy with it? Can we, that is, uncover a consensus position?

I am driven to ask this question for two reasons primarily. Practical questions cannot be brought to decision normally without such an effort, so the search for consensus is a critical part of a society that makes decisions through debatelike processes. The students need to learn the give-and-take of *phronesis* in action. The other reason is that two or several positions on a disputed issue are seldom equally good— that is, usually one position can claim more or better good reasons than all the other possible stances. If possible, I want us to find the best position on the issue, "best" being defined here as for now drawing the assent of most of the class. (Rational dissent, of course, always occurs. Consensus is never 100 percent, nor should it be.)

Let me take for illustration the issue I thought would surely stump us—abortion, which one of my classes at Texas A & M debated at length and with ingenuity, and which ended with the class divided in much the same way and roughly in the same proportion as polls suggest the general American populace is divided.

There is, of course, no method for reaching consensus, no mechanical calculus for tallying up good reasons and announcing a winner. We are not judging a debate contest via a flow pad, but rather trying to reason our way toward a position that most of us find more illuminating and convincing than any other position.

What we did was make a list of points that were either never in dispute or no longer in serious dispute. For example, the anti-abortion side had already, under the pressure of points raised in class by the other side, conceded that making abortion illegal had unacceptable consequences: abortion would not thereby stop; we would return to the days of amateur and do-it-yourself abortions, with additional loss of life and drastically negative health consequences in too many cases; relatively well-to-do women would simply fly to countries where abortion is legal, leaving the relatively disadvantaged to break the law at home; and, although the logic of the anti-abortion position drove its proponents to consider the woman who had had an abortion a first-degree murderer and the doctor an accessory, most could not follow this logic through to impose the kind of penalties customarily imposed for the crime.

The pro-abortion side had had its difficulties, too, of course: they were distressed by the annual body count of dead fetuses; they had shifted uneasily in their seats when the other side had talked about the assembly-line inhumanity of some of the abortion clinics; and they did not know what to say, except to point to the still worse consequences of illegal abortion, when the long-term consequences of legal abortion came to light, especially the psychological distress for many women.

As we listed and pondered the points of agreement, slowly a consensus position did emerge, which eventually almost 80 percent of the class said they could accept: that abortion should remain legal, but that those seeking one should undergo thorough counseling before it should be permitted. This position had its drawbacks too, but as one of the students said, summing up the appeal, perhaps, of the consensus position: "You can't call it pro-choice if a woman is un-informed or rushes into having an abortion before she has a chance to think about it."

"There is violence in learning."

I am aware that the practice of hermeneutical rhetoric as I have described it here is hardly unique. In different ways, many composition teachers are already practicing hermeneutical rhetoric. At least I think I have found it even among people who write about teaching writing out of theories that diverge from my own. At most, then, this chapter may have contributed to a better understanding of what many composition teachers are trying to do already.

I will conclude both this chapter and this book with a paragraph from Peter Elbow, who, so far as I know, never invokes hermeneutics, yet expresses its view of learning about as well as it can be expressed:

> In Piaget's terms learning involves both assimilation and accom-modation. Part of the job is to get the subject matter to bend and deform so that it fits inside the learner. . . . Just as important is the necessity for the learner to bend and deform himself so that he can

> fit himself around the subject without doing violence to it. Good
> learning is not a matter of finding a happy medium where both
> parties are transformed as little as possible. Rather both parties
> must be maximally transformed—in a sense deformed. There is
> violence in learning. (1988, 223)

Isn't this precisely what Kinneavy means when he says that composing processes are hermeneutical circles, within which "both object and
forestructure may require radical alterations, even transformations"
(1987, 7)? Whether we are drawing on Piaget or Heidegger or someone
else, the dialectic of engaged, authentic teaching remains much the
same, a kind of controlled violence in the service of Kenneth Burke's
motto from *A Grammar of Motives,* "*Ad bellum purificandum,*" toward the
purification of war, the idea being not to eliminate conflict, but to make
it a contest of words rather than bullets, ultimately cooperative, a
struggling together in our differences to find what is true for us now.
This is the place worth being and human being's best projection of
itself from the dialogue that we are.

Suggested Readings

For the uninitiated, probably the most accessible general introduction to hermeneutics is still Richard E. Palmer's 1969 volume, *Hermeneutics: Interpretation Theory in Schleiermacher, Dilthey, Heidegger, and Gadamer*. The best recent alternative is Kurt Mueller-Vollmer's *The Hermeneutics Reader* (1989), which has an excellent introduction and offers something Palmer does not, substantial texts from outstanding contributors to the hermeneutical tradition from the eighteenth century on. The bibliography is also worth consulting.

The best brief introduction to philosophical hermeneutics is the volume by that name (1976), edited by David E. Linge, a collection of essays translated from Gadamer's *Kleine Schriften*. In my opinion, Linge's introduction to this volume is the best brief exposition of ontological hermeneutics in English.

If one wishes to drink deep, the next step is to plunge into Gadamer's *Truth and Method* (1960; first English translation, 1975; second revised edition, 1989). Consult Joel C. Weinsheimer's *Gadamer's Hermeneutics: A Reading of Truth and Method* (1985), a detailed exposition and commentary that follows the book, section by section.

For Heidegger, probably the best place to start is *Basic Writings* (1977a), a collection of essays from early and late Heidegger, which includes the "General Introduction" to *Being and Time*. For the reading of *Being and Time* (1962) itself, W. J. Richardson's commentary (1964) is more than helpful—for most readers, it is essential.

For Ricoeur, whose philosophy is always hermeneutical but far more than hermeneutics, probably the best book for the beginner is *Interpretation Theory: Discourse and the Surplus of Meaning* (1976). A more substantial collection of his essays dealing with hermeneutics is found in the volume *Paul Ricoeur: Hermeneutics and the Human Sciences* (1981), translated and edited by John B. Thompson.

The secondary literature on Heidegger, Gadamer, and Ricoeur, on general hermeneutics and philosophical hermeneutics in particular, is vast and, with each year, growing even vaster. No one can read all the available material in English, much less in German, French, and Italian, the major other languages with a hermeneutical literature. I will simply list a few of the books I have found most helpful: *Hermeneutics and Modern Philosophy,* edited by Brice R. Wachterhauser (1986); *Hermeneutics and Praxis,* edited by Robert Hollinger (1985); *Critical Hermeneutics,* by John B. Thompson (1981); *Hermeneutics: Questions and Prospects,* edited by Gary Shapiro and Alan Sica (1984); *Radical Hermeneutics: Repetition, Deconstruction, and the Hermeneutic Project,* by John D. Caputo (1987); and *Dialogue and Deconstruction: The Gadamer-Derrida Encounter,* edited by Diane P. Michelfelder and Richard E. Palmer (1989).

A few last suggestions. At some point it is helpful to try to see hermeneutics within the major alternatives of contemporary philosophy. The best book for this purpose is *After Philosophy: End or Transformation?* edited by Kenneth Baynes, James Bohman, and Thomas McCarthy (1987). Also be on the lookout for more contributions to hermeneutical rhetoric. As I was finishing this study, the Modern Language Association asked me to review the typescript of a collection of essays on composition studies, several of which are ambitious and intelligent explorations of hermeneutics and rhetoric. It is a safe bet that we have just begun the task of rethinking rhetoric hermeneutically.

Glossary

Being-as-event: In traditional, Western philosophy from the ancient Greeks on, being usually means essence, the unchanging features of something that make it what it is. Or being means the Being of beings—God, the *Logos*. In modern, process philosophies, however, being is linked to time and history and becomes immanent, dynamic. Truth is no longer the eternal or fixed amid the flux of events, but rather an event itself, whatever the language of a particular time and place reveals. In philosophical hermeneutics, one of the many recent process philosophies, Being is tradition, what is handed down to us, and truth is *aletheia* (disclosure, unhiddenness). That is, we *are* our heritage, and truth happens in our language through the process of talking and writing and by reflection, by talking and writing about what has been said and written.

Consciousness of effective history: Coined by Hans-Georg Gadamer in his most important philosophical work, *Truth and Method,* the phrase designates an awareness of the sources of our being. Everyone is the product of "effective history"; tradition has us (rather than we it) in that we (at first uncritically) internalize the authoritative voices of our past. But not everyone is conscious of effective history, capable of rendering some account of his or her leading assumptions and concepts. Such consciousness of the sources of one's own being has to be cultivated to understand why we understand ourselves and the world as we do. Part of what intellectual maturity means, consciousness of effective history encourages openness to other traditions in and outside our own culture.

Dasein: A key concept in Martin Heidegger's *Being and Time, Dasein* is usually translated as "human existence" or "human-being-in-the-world." It is characterized by finitude, by historical existence within the limitations of a definite time and place, and by fallenness, inauthentic existence, the tendency to be absorbed into the everyday and the trivial. Authentic existence gains its urgency from confronting finitude as death; its task is caring and questioning without assurances, in not knowing about absolutes and ultimates, and without pretense to know.

Fusion of horizons: Another key notion from Gadamer's *Truth and Method,* fusion of horizons describes what happens in good conversation or dialogue. We begin in difference, with the various viewpoints of the participants toward the topic being discussed. Our horizons "fuse" in the sense that we come to understand the viewpoints of the other participants, and as all viewpoints are modified and enlarged by each other. "Fusion" here is a metaphor, not actually, even when consensus is achieved, a complete identity. That is, we leave the conversation also in difference, but with an increased mutual understanding and common ground.

Hermeneutics of tradition or trust: Paul Ricoeur used this category to characterize philosophical hermeneutics (among other ways of reading), contrasting its approach with the "hermeneutics of suspicion," the theory and practice of interpretation exemplified in Nietzsche, Freud, and Marx. The hermeneutics of tradition holds that "the text must be allowed to speak" (Gadamer), that what it says should be permitted to challenge our own assumptions and beliefs. The hermeneutics of suspicion views tradition as the source of bondage and error, as something to be reinterpreted in the light of a more advanced understanding superior to it. While Gadamer aims for a fusion of horizons through dialogue with a text, the hermeneutics of suspicion aims to demystify and deconstruct. Ricoeur argued that these two modes of interpretation are complementary rather than dichotomous; at present they seem alienated from one another—on the one hand, German hermeneutics, on the other, French neostructuralism—and not much effort to bring them together.

Phronesis: A Greek concept important in *Truth and Method* and difficult to translate, it is roughly equivalent to "practical judgment." Gadamer opposes it to method (algorithmic procedure) and calculation. That is, some problems and questions may be solved or answered by scientific or technical means. An engineer, for example, could study a proposed design for a bridge and say whether it could withstand certain weights and stresses. But no sheerly calculative procedure could decide whether the bridge should be built at all. Such decisions belong to argument and counterargument, to rhetoric and hermeneutics. The ability to say or do the right thing amid uncertainty and controversy is the art of practical judgment. Gadamer holds that a hermeneutical education centered in the give-and-take of dialogue best develops *phronesis.*

Prejudice: A word now with only negative connotations, it means, literally, "prejudgment." In *Truth and Method* Gadamer attempts to rehabilitate the concept. First, following Heidegger's discussion of preunderstanding in *Being and Time,* he argues that prejudice cannot be eliminated or set aside. We always live and think within a certain horizon of practices, meanings, values, and preferences. Second, he demonstrates that bias or prejudice enables experience itself. Not only is prejudgment unavoidable, but it is also positive in the sense that our understanding of ourselves and the world—our whole orientation—depends on it. Third, and finally, instead of attempting to devalue or eliminate prejudice, Gadamer makes reflection on prejudice the primary concern of hermeneutical dialogue, the end of which is not to overcome prejudice, but to distinguish enabling from disabling prejudice.

Works Cited

Aristotle. 1932. *The Rhetoric of Aristotle*. Edited by Lane Cooper. Englewood Cliffs, N.J.: Prentice-Hall, Inc.

Baynes, Kenneth, James Bohman, and Thomas McCarthy, eds. 1987. *After Philosophy: End or Transformation?* Cambridge: Massachusetts Institute of Technology Press.

Berlin, James A. 1987. *Rhetoric and Reality: Writing Instruction in American Colleges, 1900–1985*. Carbondale: Southern Illinois University Press.

———. 1988a. "Contemporary Composition: The Major Pedagogical Theories." In *The Writing Teacher's Sourcebook*, 2d ed., edited by Gary Tate and Edward P. J. Corbett, 47–59. New York: Oxford University Press.

———. 1988b. "Rhetoric and Ideology in the Writing Class." *College English* 50:477–94.

Bernstein, Richard J. 1986. "From Hermeneutics to Praxis." In *Hermeneutics and Modern Philosophy*, edited by Brice R. Wachterhauser, 87–110. Albany: State University of New York Press.

Booth, Wayne C. 1974. *Modern Dogma and the Rhetoric of Assent*. Notre Dame, Ind.: University of Notre Dame Press.

Burke, Kenneth. 1965. *Permanence and Change: An Anatomy of Purpose*, 2d ed. Indianapolis: Bobbs-Merrill Co.

———. 1969a. *A Grammar of Motives*. Berkeley: University of California Press.

———. 1969b. *A Rhetoric of Motives*. Berkeley: University of California Press.

Caputo, John D. 1987. *Radical Hermeneutics: Repetition, Deconstruction, and the Hermeneutic Project*. Bloomington: Indiana University Press.

Crowley, Sharon. 1989. *A Teacher's Introduction to Deconstruction*. Urbana, Ill.: National Council of Teachers of English.

Crusius, Timothy W. 1989. *Discourse: A Critique and Synthesis of Major Theories*. New York: Modern Language Association.

Derrida, Jacques. 1987. "The Ends of Man." In *After Philosophy: End or Transformation?* edited by Kenneth Baynes, James Bohman, and Thomas McCarthy, 125–58. Cambridge: Massachusetts Institute of Technology Press.

———. 1989. "Structure, Sign, and Play in the Discourse of the Human Sciences." In *The Critical Tradition: Classical Texts and Contemporary Trends*, edited by David H. Richter, 959–70. New York: St. Martin's Press.

Dreyfus, Hubert L. 1985. "Holism and Hermeneutics." In *Hermeneutics and Praxis*, edited by Robert Hollinger, 227–47. Notre Dame, Ind.: University of Notre Dame Press.

Elbow, Peter. 1988. "Embracing Contraries in the Teaching Process." In *The Writing Teacher's Sourcebook*, 2d ed., edited by Gary Tate and Edward P. J. Corbett, 219–31. New York: Oxford University Press.

Emig, Janet. 1988. "Writing as a Mode of Learning." In *The Writing Teacher's Sourcebook*, 2d ed., edited by Gary Tate and Edward P. J. Corbett, 85–91. New York: Oxford University Press.

Gadamer, Hans-Georg. 1976a. *Hegel's Dialectic: Five Hermeneutical Studies*. Translated by P. Christopher Smith. New Haven, Conn.: Yale University Press.

———. 1976b. *Philosophical Hermeneutics*. Translated and edited by David E. Linge. Berkeley: University of California Press.

———. 1986. "On the Scope and Function of Hermeneutical Reflection." Translated by G. B. Hess and R. E. Palmer. In *Hermeneutics and Modern Philosophy*, edited by Brice R. Wachterhauser, 277–99. Albany: State University of New York Press.

———. 1989a. "Rhetoric, Hermeneutics, and the Critique of Ideology: Metacritical Comments on *Truth and Method*." In *The Hermeneutics Reader: Texts of the German Tradition from the Enlightenment to the Present*, edited by Kurt Mueller-Vollmer, 274–92. New York: Continuum.

———. 1989b. *Truth and Method*, 2d ed. Translated by Garrett Barden and John Cumming; revised translation by Joel Weinsheimer and Donald G. Marshall. New York: Crossroads Publishing Company.

Habermas, Jürgen. 1975. *Legitimation Crisis*. Translated by Thomas McCarthy. Boston: Beacon Press.

———. 1986. "A Review of Gadamer's *Truth and Method*." Translated by Fred Dallmayr and Thomas McCarthy. In *Hermeneutics and Modern Philosophy*, edited by Brice R. Wachterhauser, 243–76. Albany: State University of New York Press.

———. 1987. "Philosophy as Stand-In and Interpreter." In *After Philosophy: End or Transformation?* edited by Kenneth Baynes, James Bohman, and Thomas McCarthy, 296–315. Cambridge: Massachusetts Institute of Technology Press.

———. 1989. "On Hermeneutics' Claim to Universality." In *The Hermeneutics Reader: Texts of the German Tradition from the Enlightenment to the Present*, edited by Kurt Mueller-Vollmer, 294–319. New York: Continuum.

Hegel, G. W. F. 1969. *Hegel's Science of Logic*. Translated by A. V. Miller. London: Allen and Unwin. (This edition is a reprint by Humanities Press, New York.)

Heidegger, Martin. 1962. *Being and Time*. Translated by John Macquarrie and Edward Robinson. New York: Harper and Row.

———. 1977a. *Basic Writings from Being and Time (1927) to the Task of Thinking (1964)*, edited by David Farrell Krell. New York: Harper and Row.

———. 1977b. *The Question Concerning Technology and Other Essays*. Translated by William Lovitt. New York: Harper and Row.

Hollinger, Robert, ed. 1985. *Hermeneutics and Praxis*. Notre Dame, Ind.: University of Notre Dame Press.

Kinneavy, James L. 1979. "The Relation of the Whole to the Part in Interpretative Theory and in the Composing Process." In *Linguistics,*

Stylistics, and the Teaching of Composition, edited by Donald McQuade, 1–23. Akron, Ohio: Department of English, University of Akron.

———. 1987. "The Process of Writing: A Philosophical Base in Hermeneutics." *Journal of Advanced Composition* 7:1–9.

Lentricchia, Frank. 1983. *Criticism and Social Change.* Chicago: University of Chicago Press.

Linge, David E. 1976. "Editor's Introduction." In *Philosophical Hermeneutics,* translated and edited by David E. Linge, xi–lviii. Berkeley: University of California Press.

Lyotard, Jean-François. 1984. *The Postmodern Condition.* Minneapolis: University of Minnesota Press.

Michelfelder, Diane P., and Richard E. Palmer, eds. 1989. *Dialogue and Deconstruction: The Gadamer-Derrida Encounter.* Albany: State University of New York Press.

Mueller-Vollmer, Kurt, ed. 1989. *The Hermeneutics Reader: Texts of the German Tradition from the Enlightenment to the Present.* New York: Continuum.

Murray, Donald M. 1988. "The Listening Eye: Reflections on the Writing Conference." In *The Writing Teacher's Sourcebook,* 2d ed., edited by Gary Tate and Edward P. J. Corbett, 232–37. New York: Oxford University Press.

Neel, Jasper P. 1988. *Plato, Derrida, and Writing.* Carbondale: Southern Illinois University Press.

Nozick, Robert. 1981. *Philosophical Explanations.* Cambridge, Mass.: Harvard University Press.

Palmer, Richard E. 1969. *Hermeneutics: Interpretation Theory in Schleiermacher, Dilthey, Heidegger and Gadamer.* Evanston, Ill.: Northwestern University Press.

Perelman, Chaim, and L. Olbrechts-Tyteca. 1969. *The New Rhetoric: A Treatise on Argumentation.* Translated by John Wilkinson and Purcell Weaver. Notre Dame, Ind.: University of Notre Dame Press.

Phelps, Louise W. 1988. *Composition as a Human Science: Contributions to the Self-Understanding of a Discipline.* New York: Oxford University Press.

———, ed. 1983. *Ricoeur and Rhetoric.* Special issue, *Pre/Text* 4.

Polanyi, Michael. 1962. *Personal Knowledge: Towards a Post-Critical Philosophy.* Chicago: University of Chicago Press.

Richardson, W. J. 1964. *Martin Heidegger: From Phenomenology to Thought.* The Hague: Nijhoff.

Ricoeur, Paul. 1970. *Freud and Philosophy: An Essay on Interpretation.* Translated by Denis Savage. New Haven, Conn.: Yale University Press.

———. 1976. *Interpretation Theory: Discourse and the Surplus of Meaning.* Fort Worth: Texas Christian University Press.

———. 1981. *Paul Ricoeur: Hermeneutics and the Human Sciences: Essays on Language, Action, and Interpretation.* Edited and translated by John B. Thompson. New York: Cambridge University Press.

Shapiro, Gary, and Alan Sica. 1984. *Hermeneutics: Questions and Prospects.* Amherst: University of Massachusetts Press.

Thompson, John B. 1981. *Critical Hermeneutics: A Study in the Thought of Paul Ricoeur and Jurgen Habermas.* New York: Cambridge University Press.

Vickers, Brian. 1988. *In Defence of Rhetoric.* Oxford: Clarendon Press.

Weinsheimer, Joel C. 1985. *Gadamer's Hermeneutics: A Reading of Truth and Method.* New Haven, Conn.: Yale University Press.

Index

Author

Timothy W. Crusius is associate professor of English at Southern Methodist University and director of composition. The author of *Discourse: A Critique and Synthesis of Recent Theories* (MLA, 1989) and numerous articles on Kenneth Burke, he is currently writing a first-year text, *The Aims of Argument.* His research centers in the overlap between rhetoric and philosophy, especially in postmodernism.